Raging Winds Roaring Sea

Robert Parsons

Raging Winds Roaring Sea

Robert Parsons

St. John's, Newfoundland
2000

© 2000, Robert C. Parsons

Le Conseil des Arts du Canada | The Canada Council for the Arts

We acknowledge the support of *the Canada Council for the Arts* for our publishing program.

We acknowledge the financial support of the Government of Canada through the book publishing industry Development Program (BPIDP) for our publishing activities.

All rights reserved. No part of this work covered by the copyrights hereon may be reproduced or used in any form or by any means—graphic, electronic or mechanical—without the prior written permission of the publisher. Any requests for photocopying, recording, taping or information storage and retrieval systems of any part of this book shall be directed in writing to the Canadian Reprography Collective, One Yonge Street, Suite 1900, Toronto, Ontario M5E 1E5.

Cover art: David Peckford

∞ Printed on acid-free paper

Published by
CREATIVE BOOK PUBLISHING
a division of 10366 Newfoundland Limited
a Robinson-Blackmore Printing & Publishing associated company
P.O. Box 8660, St. John's, Newfoundland A1B 3T7
Printed in Canada by:
ROBINSON-BLACKMORE PRINTING & PUBLISHING

Canadian Cataloguing in Publication Data

Parsons, Robert Charles, 1944 –

Raging winds, roaring sea

Ibcludes index.
ISBN 1-894294-29-7

1. Shipwrecks—Newfoundland—History.
2. Newfoundland—History, Local.   I. Title.

FC2170.S5P3718   2000   971.8   C00-901580-9
G525.P372   2000

I dedicate
Raging Winds...Roaring Sea
to publisher Don Morgan:
He first showed his faith in me
in 1990

Table of Contents

Author's Notes and Introduction

Over the past two or three years I have had several sea stories published in various local and provincial newspapers and magazines. In the fall of 1998 (after my book *Committed to the Deep* was in hands of the publisher and *In Peril on the Sea* was developing), I took those stories and compiled them into one collection.

Throughout the next year, as my other stories (such as "Pilley's Island Launch, Long Island Demise" — *Evening Telegram* January 19, 2000) appeared in various publications, each was arranged into the collection. That accounts for about half the stories in *Raging Winds...Roaring Sea*; the other tales of the sea appear for the first time in this collection. These were researched and written since early 1999. There is the chance then that you may have read some of these stories in a newspaper or magazine. Of course the benefit of buying this book is that you get all the stories, the few previously published and those as of now unpublished, under one cover.

What kinds of stories are in this book? Some are mysteries of the sea. Others describe the hardships and the uncommon sea adventures our seafaring ancestors endured. One or two chapters in *Raging Winds...Roaring Sea* can't really be classed as "stories": for example, Susanna Tucker's account of sailing to Oporto in 1930 aboard a small schooner. I believed it was too important and unusual to leave out and I hope you, the reader, will agree. Many selections are of obscure Newfoundland sea disasters; others are more widely-known tragedies but written from a new perspective. Where possible, I gave the names, the faces, the kin of our island pioneers for, not only is this valuable for our descendants, but injects a personality, a life, an authenticity into past events.

Each story is introduced with notes and personal observations — a paragraph or two saying where and when each sea tale originated, who inspired it, or why and how each was written. These background notes are not essential to the enjoyment of a sea story, but I hope you, dear reader, will bear with me.

As I worked with the material for *Raging Winds...Roaring Sea* I often saw stories and instances where the North Atlantic changed almost instantly from a calm and quiet workplace to a seascape filled with high wind and dangerous whitecaps. There were (and will be) seamen who were suddenly faced with wreck or the terror of being thrown into the raging ocean or onto jagged rocks. It is with little wonder then there are many versions of mariner's prayers —from the short but powerful, "Oh God, Thy sea is so great, and my boat is so small, Amen" to the more eloquent supplication given on page xiii of this book.

It is from that prayer the title *Raging Winds...Roaring Sea* was chosen and it reflects the theme of most stories in this collection. Each marine misadventure was influenced, like me, by that great element of nature always stamping at our doorstep and by the supreme being who shapes the winds, the seas, and human destiny.

Come back with me now, back to the days when our forefathers plied the ocean in their quest to wrest a living from the ocean that surrounds our province.

—Robert C. Parsons
32 Pearson Place
Grand Bank, NF
November 2000

E-mail: robert.parsons2@nf.sympatico.ca
Website: www3.nf.sympatico.ca/robert.parsons2/

Acknowledgements

Lance Blackmore — Port Union/Grand Bank
Allison (Edwards) Brenton — Lawn/Grand Bank
Edith Burrage — New Perlican
Elizabeth Bursey — St. Philip's
Sam Carter — Greenspond
Norman and son
    Roy Chaytor — St. John's
Frances (Baird) Cole — St. John's
Shirley Crewe — Goose Bay, Labrador/
    Glovertown

Denyce (Solo) Deters — Edmonton, AB
Tom Douglas — Fortune
John Edgecombe — Catalina/Holyrood
Barbara (Tucker) Foley — Hamilton, ON
Gary Forward — Tizzard's Harbour
Ralph Getson, curator — Fisheries Museum of the Atlantic
Margaret (Strickland) Grant — Mount Pearl
Llewellyn Grimes — Herring Neck
Hon. Chief Justice
    T. Alex Hickman — St. John's/Grand Bank
Mary (Barnes) Hillier — Grand Bank
Boyd & Byron Holloway,
    Megan Walsh — Spanish Room
Clayton Hutchings — Sechelt, BC
Dorothy Kavanagh and family — Hartford, Connecticut, USA
Alfreda (Smith) Marsh — Owen Sound, ON
Austin Murphy — Lawn/Toronto
Joe Osmond — Port aux Basques/
    Powell River, BC

Lew and son Scott Parsons — Ottawa/Portugal Cove, C.B.
Russell Patten — Ottawa/Grand Bank
Anna Belle Peddle — Bloomfield
Peter Perham — Carp, ON
Floyd and Carl Priddle — Milltown, Bay d'Espoir
Capt. Joseph Prim — St. John's
Alan Rogers — Fair Island/Centerville
Charles A. Rose — St. John's/Port Union/
    Grand Bank

Janet Schlievert — Cambridge, Ontario
Roberta (Misuraca) Sheedy — Gloucester, Mass., USA

xi

Harold Simms	Norwell, Mass., USA
Kim (Parsons) Squires	Portugal Cove
Them Days (Doris Saunders, ed.)	Goose Bay, Labrador
Maude Senior	Port Elizabeth/Red Harbour
Susanna (Douglas) Tucker	Westmount, NS
Bruce Warr	Robert's Arm
Ivy Tong White	Greenspond/St. John's
James White	Spaniard's Bay/Chamberlains

I appreciate the help and co-operation of the staff at the Newfoundland Reference Section A.C. Hunter Library; the Marine Archives, Elizabeth Avenue, St. John's; and the Centre for Newfoundland Studies/Archives, Memorial University.

To those who loaned or supplied me with photographs of schooners or seamen, I am deeply grateful for the opportunity of re-producing your photos for this work. I have made every effort to identify rightful owners and to obtain proper permission to reproduce them. If any errors occur in this regard or in the information given in the text please notify the author and efforts to correct them will be made in any subsequent editions.

I am indebted to many other individuals who contributed a name, a fact, an idea, a section of a story, a suggestion or hint of a marine misadventure; if you are not acknowledged in the above list, the omission was an oversight and unintentional.

William Chapman read my early manuscript and gave perceptive advice. To other manuscript readers and editors, a thank you. Don Morgan and Heather Tucker gave advice about certain key elements as I was preparing the final draft. I would be remiss if I didn't acknowledge, once again, the resources, expertise and general co-operation of Jack Keeping, Fortune.

"O most glorious and gracious Lord God, who dwellest in heaven, but beholdest all things below; Look down, we beseech thee, and hear us, calling out of the depth of misery, and out of the jaws of this death, which is now ready to swallow us up: Save, Lord, or else we perish. The living, the living shall praise thee. O send thy word of command to rebuke the raging winds and the roaring sea; that we, being delivered from this distress, may live to serve thee, and to glorify thy Name all the days of our life. Hear, Lord, and save us, for the infinite merits of our blessed Saviour, thy Son, our Lord Jesus Christ. Amen"

From *The American Episcopal Church Book of Common Prayer, Prayers to be Used in Storms at Sea*

The basic details for this story came from old newspapers (*Evening Telegram* September 18, 1891 and the *Twillingate Sun* September 19, 1891.) Generally these news items are short, factual and quite often do not provide crew names. Without background information of the families involved, such sea stories would lack a human or intimate element. To this end I am grateful to Shirley Crewe, Goose Bay, whose great-grandfather, Joseph Ings, was the "one survivor." Joseph and Alfreda Marsh of Owen Sound, Ontario, supplied details on *Blossom's* captain and on the Union Jack, the sole object preserved from the wreck scene. Both correspondents certainly demonstrate the spirit of Newfoundland people who, through their wonderful tradition of re-telling family stories, have not let the memory of ships like the *Blossom* or the seamen disappear. I submitted this story to the *Downhomer* for publication where it appeared in the April 2000 issue.

1 One Survivor to Tell the Tale

Purcell's Harbour, Twillingate, New World Island

*I*n the early years of the salt cod fishery, independent vessel owners in the towns and islands of Notre Dame Bay took their ships to the lucrative Labrador grounds. They sailed there in small schooners which enterprising young men usually built themselves. Joseph Marsh of Purcell's Harbour was one of these hard-working individuals. In 1883, at age thirty-two, he built his own vessel, the thirty ton *Blossom*, and voyaged to the Labrador coast for the summer/early fall fishery.

But such ventures where man had to contend with unexpected storms, a rocky coast and a long voyage were not without tragedy. The *Blossom*, under the command of Marsh with his six crew, was lost about midnight of Tuesday, September 15, 1891. The six were James Witt, George Gidge, Joseph Ings, Obadiah Vining, Arthur Langdown and a girl,

Priscilla Langdown (often spelled Langdon). In those days, it was the custom to carry a girl cook on voyages to the Labrador. Other family sources claim Francis Marsh, brother to Joseph, was also on board although local papers make no mention of him. There was one survivor, Joseph Ings.

Most of the crew belonged to Purcell's Harbour, a community located about six kilometres southeast of Twillingate. Purcell's Harbour opens on Main Tickle, which separates South Twillingate Island from New World Island. In 1911 when the census first listed Purcell's Harbour as distinct from Twillingate, its population was seventy-seven; today it stands at around one hundred people.

The *Blossom* left White's Arm on the French Shore under full sail in a light northeast breeze. About eight o'clock in the evening of September 15, the wind increased to a strong gale. Captain Marsh had all sails lowered and tied down and *Blossom* sped along under bare poles, or with no canvas aloft. That evening the men listened and watched to determine their position. They saw land and white breakers just before twelve that night. Immediately the captain ordered the sails up in an attempt to keep the schooner off the rocks, but it was too late! She struck the sunkers of Gull Island Cove, in the Bay of Exploits, three miles above Black Island, near sea lanes once known as Exploits Ship's Run.

When *Blossom* hit a ledge at the base of a steep cliff, the jibboom and bowsprit were carried away and one man went over the side with it, never to be seen again. She drifted off slightly from the ledge; seas rolled across her deck and another crewman and the girl, Priscilla Langdown were swept over the side by a large comber that nearly engulfed the schooner.

Joseph Ings jumped for the rocks and a sea carried him onto the slippery crags beneath a cliff. He later said the girl was right behind him ready to jump, but when *Blossom* struck she was thrown back as she prepared to jump or before Ings could help her.

Ings climbed up higher on the craggy outcrop and stopped because the overhang was so tilted he could climb no further. Looking back to watch his vessel, he could see the captain and two men on deck working to keep the little ship from the ledges. About fifteen minutes later a heavy sea broke over *Blossom*, smashing her to pieces against the ledge and carrying away the remaining three men. Nothing was seen of them again.

Ings remained on the cliff until daylight. He knew there were houses about a quarter of a mile away, but his position was such that he could climb no farther up the cliff nor could he go down and around it. About eight A.M. several men appeared on the scene above the cliff. He called and they answered, but high seas prevented them from rowing to him in a small boat.

Eventually they lowered a rope which Ings tied around his body. When he saw a lull in the waves he jumped into the sea. His rescuers pulled him about one hundred feet through the water and over rocks to safety. No bodies were recovered. Very little wreckage — two or three casks of oil and a trunk — drifted ashore.

Ings was one of six boys born to Thomas Ings and Lydia (Stuckless) in Friday's Bay — since renamed Hillgrade — New World Island. Joseph Ings married Dorcas Rice in 1886 and had two daughters: Dulcie and Veonie. Dulcie married William Crewe of Glovertown and they had two girls and three boys: Evelyn, Eileen, Harold, Eric and Wallace. Shirley Crewe, the daughter of Eric, supplied the background information on her ancestors Thomas and Joseph Ings.

In later years, Joseph Ings talked very little about the traumatic experience of watching his shipmates drown, his desperate climb up the cliff, and his long, cold wait for rescue. He did recall Captain Marsh, a spiritual man who was a lay reader in the Wesleyan church and taught Sunday school, singing the chorus of a hymn as he worked to save his ship and crew:

"With his loving hand to guide, Let the clouds above me roll,
And the billows in their fury dash around me,

3

I can brave the wildest storm..."

Owner and master of *Blossom* Joseph Marsh, age thirty-two, was born in Purcell's Harbour on Twillingate Island. At the time of his death he was married to Joanna (Anstey) and had four children, Effie May, Matilda, Winnifred and William Marsh — William served for many years as an officer in the Salvation Army.

Today the only physical reminders that this ship ever existed are a brief clipping in an old newspaper and a tattered and torn but otherwise well-preserved Union Jack. Apparently, as recounted in family lore, someone from Black Island where *Blossom* was wrecked, salvaged the ship's flag, or it may have come from the trunk found at the scene. The flag was eventually presented to William Marsh who in turn passed to Joe Marsh, the grandson and namesake of *Blossom's* captain.

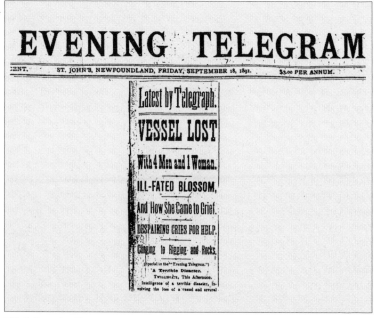

This is how the *Evening Telegram* reported the disaster in its September 18, 1891 newspaper.

This story was published in the *Evening Telegram*, May 23, 1999; it would not have been possible except for the grand-daughter of Joe Solo and the marvel of the Internet. Three months before its publication, Denyce (Solo) Deters wrote me to enquire if I had any knowledge of the wreck of S.S. *Marvale* which had happened near her grandfather's hometown. We shared information when I sent clippings of the loss of the steamer and the auction of her cargo and Denyce provided a biography of entrepreneur Solo.

This story of a Newfoundland family name bears out the need to know more about our roots and origins. In recent years there has been a resurgence of people looking to Newfoundland to re-discover family history, genealogy and to touch and to walk in the communities, some since abandoned, where ancestors once lived. F. Scott Fitzgerald understood the search to re-discover ourselves when he wrote, "So we beat on, boats against the current, bourne back ceaselessly into the past."

2   Solo of the Cape Shore

St. Shott's, Branch, Cape Shore

Solo is indeed a rare surname in Newfoundland. Seary's book of Newfoundland family names lists Solo as "of unascertained origin." Today most Solo families live in the Corner Brook area, but the name had its Newfoundland origins on the Cape Shore. The name and its connections with the wreck of the CPR liner *Marvale* in 1923 are intertwined — a part of this island's mosaic of the sea.

Sulieman Yousif Saleh, born in 1888 at Majdal Shams, Golan Heights, Syria, came to Newfoundland in 1912. A peddlar, as were many of his countrymen, Sulieman was a Druzi;* the Druze, the people, are an ethnic and religious sect

_____

* One person is referred to as a Druzi

Photo courtesy Denyce Deters

Joe Solo, who once lived at Branch, then moved to Corner Brook.

in the Middle East associated with the Moslem faith. The Druze pronunciation of Saleh sounds similar to the word, Solo; thus Sulieman's last name became Solo.

Sulieman settled in and naturalized quite well on the Cape Shore, an area extending from Cape St. Marys to Placentia. In 1917 he married Agnes Foley of Little Barachois, Placentia Bay and settled in Branch. He established and ran two general stores. By then his name had anglicized to Simon Joseph "Joe" Solo — easier to pronounce — and the twelve children born to the couple became Solo. He became a naturalized citizen of Newfoundland in 1920.

Solo prospered, selling various types of merchandise on the southern Avalon, and made more than an adequate living for his family. He is fondly remembered; today a Cape Shore Development Association tourism brochure includes a statement encouraging visitors to come and see the area where "...Joe Solo the peddler made his fortune from a wrecked cargo of cotton thread."

Solo did indeed sell thread, which came in large reels. This thread had been salvaged from *Marvale*'s wreck at St. Shott's. No doubt Solo sold other commodities from the same wreck, but thread is the item for which he is best remembered. His prosperity was built on the loss of the steamer *Marvale*.

Marvale Ashore near St. Shott's—Newfoundland's first news of the shipwreck came at five pm on May 21, 1923 when operator Kerton at Cape Race wired St. John's to say:

"S.S. *Marvale* just struck Cape Freels Rock, holds flooding and now heading for the beach. Requires immediate assistance; notify Minister of Shipping and advise action quickly."

That spring the seven thousand net ton *Marvale* was on her second voyage of the Montreal-Liverpool run. She had been built in 1907 at Glasgow as the *Corsican*, a sister ship to *Hesperian* and *Grampian*, owned by the Allan line. During World War One all three were troopships. As *Corsican* she had sailed into St. John's many times bringing Newfoundland soldiers home from Europe. The Victoria Cross recipient Sergeant Tommy Ricketts returned by this ship. In 1922 she was transferred along with *Victorian*, *Tunisian* and *Scotian* to the "M" class and renamed *Marvale*; others were known as *Marlock*, *Marburn* and *Marglen*.

On her final voyage she carried 200 passengers and a general cargo, mostly wheat and farm products. While off Newfoundland on May 21, 1923 *Marvale* had been steaming through thick fog all day. Tides had pulled her too near land and about four pm she ran upon Cape Freels Rock which lies one and a half miles from the nearest land, Cape Pine. In bad weather, seas constantly break over the rock, but *Marvale* struck when the weather was moderate. *Marvale*'s crew probably heard the powerful fog alarm on Freels Rock, but it was later surmised they had mistaken the blast for either the Cape Race or the Cape Pine horn.

Captain Lewis immediately wired Cape Race saying *Marvale* had backed off the rock, but her forward holds were flooding. He indicated he was going to try to beach the steamer, which was settling fast.

At 5:30 Captain Lewis reported all passengers safe and all lifeboats out. This was the last message from *Marvale*. She had been abandoned in seven fathoms of water; only her bridge deck, masts and smoke stacks showed above water. Passengers (including many small children with their parents) and crew, four hundred and thirty-six all told, rowed into St. Shott's.

The immediate concern was how to get them transferred to a larger centre. St. Shott's at this time had a population of about one hundred and had no reserves of food and shelter for such a great influx of people. Captain Lewis walked to Trepassey, fourteen miles away, to report the particulars of the wreck.

Early the next morning several ships — *Mary*, *Mapledawn*, *Susu*, *Seal* and *Cabot* — steamed to St. Shott's or Trepassey to take the passengers to a larger centre. *Seal* and *Cabot* put into St. Shotts and transferred them to Trepassey. The next day most crew travelled to St. John's on the S.S. *Susu* and special trains sent to Trepassey brought the remaining crew and passengers to the city. When S.S. *Melita*, a CPR liner bound for Liverpool but re-routed to Newfoundland, arrived in St. John's the circuitous journey of *Marvale*'s human cargo came to an end.

A Passenger's Story — Before the passengers left St. John's, Mrs. Thomas McElroy of Montreal who was travelling with her son Thomas, related her version of the wreck of *Marvale*.

We had dense fog all day and at 3:45 pm the ship crashed upon Cape Freels Rock. At the time afternoon tea was being served and the crash was felt by all on board. We soon realized that disaster had overtaken the liner.

Soon the ship listed to the starboard and then slid off the rock and steadied herself. Although the fog had been intense all day, just after the ship struck, it lifted for a few minutes and we saw land a mile off.

Captain Lewis immediately ordered the boats out and as the ship began to sink, we made preparations to abandon *Marvale*. While boats were being launched the best of order prevailed.

The Second Mate was very daring when a lifeboat, which was full of passengers, threatened to topple over. He climbed to the top of the davits and reaching out steadied the boat in time to save the occupants from being thrown into the sea.

Her story concluded with praise for the people of St. Shott's whom she had been told have always played a prominent part in all marine disasters along the coast. "(We) were received by the people and hospitably treated."

The entire complement of four hundred and thirty-six of *Marvale*'s passengers and crew had stayed in the small town on the night of May 21-22, 1923. The St. Shott's people had done their best to cope with a human flood and shared even "the last print or container of fresh butter" with their unexpected guests. According to Mrs. Thomas McElroy, all passengers voiced the opinion that their kindness should not pass unnoticed.

In the evening of May 23, tug *Hugh D*, Captain Rose, returned to St. John's. Rose figured considerable fittings could be salvaged from the wreck and it should be possible to remove the hatches to get at the bacon, ham and the large wheels of cheese in the cargo holds. J.H. Dee, representing the Customs, was requested to remain near the scene in the interests of the Department of Marine and Shipping.

By June first salvage operations finished up at the *Marvale* wreck site. Divers on the steamers *Strathcona* and *Cabot* removed the safes from the purser's room. Diver Squires opened the number two, three and four holds. He reported all cargo had gone out of the holds. Some had driven ashore; others to sea. None of the baggage in number one hold had been recovered. *Marvale* was fast breaking up on the rugged reef and in the heavy seas whipped up by a northeast wind.

Her lifeboats which had been left on the beach at St. Shott's were battered and practically useless. The final report stated if the weather held off it might be possible for divers to reach some of the valuables left in the passenger staterooms, but there was no hope of getting any more of the great quantity of cargo.

Some cargo claimed by the Wreck Commissioner was sold or dealt to local buyers and enterprising businessmen like Joe Solo, who profited greatly selling cloth and thread along the Cape Shore. In the mid-1920s Solo and his family

An advertisement for the July 9, 1923 *Daily News* notified the public of the auction of goods from the *Marvale*.

moved to Corner Brook where a considerable Syrian population lived. Several of his descendants live there today.

Often marine disasters have curious endings and the loss of *Marvale* is no exception. Several passengers and crew of *Marvale* belonged to Ireland. On June 11, while on S.S. *Graphic*

Photo courtesy Maritime Archives, Capt. Harry Stone Collection

Corsican (above), renamed *Marvale*, was wrecked near St. Shott's in May, 1923.

travelling to Belfast, they were involved in another ship-wreck. *Graphic* collided with the U.S. steamer *Balsam* off Lough, Ireland. The latter's forepeak filled with water, but she anchored in Lough and was later towed into Belfast. *Graphic* also beached on Belfast's Lough, but as in the wreck of *Marvale*, all crew and passengers survived.

As I scoured old papers looking for a particular marine event, another item of a Newfoundland tragedy appeared. This was the story of the ship *Rose*; useful not only for the details of the wreck, but also because it included names of those saved and lost, a valuable source for genealogists.

In June 2000 I received a call from an editor of the *Downhomer*, Newfoundland's folksy newspaper, who wanted a story from the Conception Bay area. I suggested the account of the loss of *Rose*. The story appeared in the August 2000 issue and, as a result of its public appearance, James White called me. Formerly of Spaniard's Bay and now residing in Chamberlains, James was a direct descendant of one of the victims of the *Rose* disaster. He brought the story forward to the present day, so to speak, when he told me what happened to the descendants of one family.

3 The Rose of Spaniard's Bay

Spaniard's Bay, Upper Island Cove, La Scie

Sometimes one can read in shipping lists various snippets of ship sinkings and of lives lost at sea. Often they are brief and bare of the details of how and why a particular shipping catastrophe occurred or who was involved. Such is this short entry found in a local publication: *"Rose. A schooner out of Spaniard's Bay. Sank with 12 aboard after striking an ice pan off La Scie June 17, 1894."*

What follows then are details on the circumstances of the wreck of the schooner *Rose*, the plight of the survivors, and the names of the unfortunate victims of a rather unheralded shipwreck originating out of Conception Bay.

Henry Gosse of Spaniard's Bay commanded the Labrador schooner *Rose*. In mid-June, 1894, he set sail for the Labrador with his crew of five or six. *Rose* also had on board several families of "freighters" heading to Labrador to live and fish for the summer. Each family — men, women and young children — carried with them food, household effects, clothing and supplies to their temporary homes at Horse Harbour on the Labrador coast. There was not much room aboard, but the voyage would only last a few days. In the fall the fishing families would return home with their catch and their household effects.

At first, the trip north for the sixty-two people aboard went well. Living quarters in the ship's hold were crowded and there was not much privacy, but that was a minor inconvenience on a voyage to the Labrador. The schooner ran before a fair breeze with light fog. But on Sunday June 17, while off the Baie Verte Peninsula, fog conditions worsened. Before sail could be shortened to reduce speed, *Rose* struck a pan of ice at four in the evening, about ten miles northeast of Tilt Cove, off the Baie Verte Peninsula.

In six minutes the schooner went to the bottom. One can only imagine the ensuing terror —mothers frantically gathering children and preparing to abandon ship, the men torn between helping family and launching the lifeboats, the crew rushing around the deck preparing lifeboats or trying to save their own lives. One eye witness describing the event said, "The consternation on board at the time was something frightful."

A minute or two after impact five men climbed out on the jibboom, jumped into the sea and managed to get on the pan of ice — the same sheet of ice that sank the ship. Many women and children were sleeping below and were literally roused from sleep by cold water pouring in. They scrambled up from below to face confusion, terror, and an uncertain death by drowning or hypothermia.

Captain Gosse wisely kept his wits about him and immediately ordered out the two boats lashed on the deck. Three men, Jacob Smith of Tilton, Solomon Gosse and Thomas Lundrigan, prepared one boat. Although filled to the point of swamping with twenty-five men, women and children, it reached a shelf of ice not too far away. While this was happening other passengers climbed in the other boat still on the deck. When water rose over the sinking *Rose*, the boat floated free of the wreckage. This group also made it onto the ice floes.

But there were not enough boats to accommodate all sixty-two aboard. Thirty people struggled in the icy water after the schooner went down. Those who could keep themselves up were rescued by the returning lifeboats, but twelve sank never to be seen again. Prospects for the survivors now stranded on a pan of ice were grim. In small groups they huddled in their wet clothes trying to keep warm, probably discussing who would attempt to reach land first. Exposure, hunger and thirst stared them in the face.

Several hours after the last survivors landed on the shelf of ice, the schooner *Irene*, belonging to Catalina and commanded by Captain Bursey, passed in the distance. Somehow the stranded people signalled and *Irene* moved in to assist the shivering castaways. Had it not been for the timely arrival of this schooner, many would likely have perished on the ice or in their attempt to reach safety. Captain Bursey landed them at Coachman's Cove and from there the group went to La Scie, a port of call for the northern coastal steamer.

On June 27, the S.S. *Virginia Lake*, while making her regular mail and passenger run from northern Newfoundland to St. John's, stopped at La Scie to take the survivors home.

Reports of the day list the eight men of the twelve drowned (the names of two women and two children are omitted). All belonged to Spaniard's Bay or Upper Island Cove: Ebenezer Gosse, John Crane Sr., James Clifford and John Coombs all of whom were married. Four were single men: Samuel Hudson, Jacob Gosse, Simon McKenzie, and Augustus Gosse. Jacob, age twenty-one, and Augustus Gosse, twenty-three, were brothers. Crane left a wife and five children; Coombs a wife and two children; Clifford, a wife and two children.

Most of the survivors were destitute. Reverend J.S. Sanderson, writing from the Parsonage in Upper Island Cove, sent an appeal to the *Evening Telegram* on June 30, 1894. He, joined later by Rev. Snow of Spaniard's Bay, asked readers for assistance in cash, food, bedding or clothing. He mentioned in particular Elijah Mercer, Eldrid Crane, John Crane Jr., William Crane, William Mercer, Josiah Mercer, Mary Margaret Drover and Alice Drover who had returned home without extra clothes and food.

Particularly distressed was the family of Thomas Lundrigan, the man who had helped get the first boat off deck. He, with his wife and five children, came home to an empty house. He had all his household effects on the *Rose* and lost every article of his material possessions, including fishing gear. Others who lost their belongings were Jacob Smith and James Chipman of Tilton; Solomon Gosse, and two men both named William Gosse of Spaniard's Bay.

Mr. G.M. Harris, a passenger on the *Virginia Lake* when the steamer brought the survivors from La Scie to Conception Bay, was likewise appalled at the desperate conditions and dire distress of the families. Harris listened to their tragic stories and agreed to help them once he reached St. John's. In a letter to the local paper, he wrote:

> The *Rose* survivors were taken to La Scie where Father Sheenan (the parish priest of Coachman's Cove) and the magistrate did all they could to assist them. One poor woman, with a family of six children, lost her husband and is in dire need of food and money. They have lost all they owned and are without a job, money, clothes and food. In fulfilment of my promise to these poor people I take the liberty of presenting their deplorable case to the public.

Not all crew and passengers were identified, but this brief look into the past — gleaned from newspaper *Twillingate Sun* of June 30, 1894, and two letters written to St. John's papers — sheds some light on the circumstances and of the people of the wreck of the schooner *Rose*. It is but one vignette, a glimpse into the trials of those bound to the sea and the exacting price the unforgiving ocean demanded.

Marine tragedies have their own footnotes and this one is no exception. Not long ago James White (named after crewman James Clifford who drowned on *Rose*) provided details

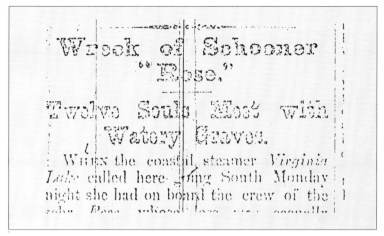

The tragedy of the *Rose* as reported in the daily papers.

of what happened to widow Catherine Clifford. When her husband was lost, Catherine (nee Smith of Bishop's Cove, Conception Bay) had two daughters, Virtue age four and Sarah Fanny, age eight. Mother and children eventually moved to Boston where the brother of James Clifford lived and worked. At Boston the two girls married, both to men of Twillingate. The surname Clifford is rare in Newfoundland today.

"You look for one thing and find another," is an old saying I've heard and have often proven its validity. Not long ago I searched the newspaper archives in St. John's looking for facts on the loss of the schooner *Flash* out of New Perlican in 1877. I did find news of the *Flash* (see story 27) but what was equally intriguing was a snippet of Newfoundland history from same time period. It involved the loss of a schooner on Newfoundland's west coast, but also hinted on the mystery of a shipwreck and the murder of Captain Rideout.

In time I worked on the new-found "ship and murder mystery" thinking that I had exhausted the basic details. Information was sparse; after all, the events happened over one hundred and twenty years ago. Then, an e-mail arrived from a distant relative of Captain Fred Rideout. This information gave a follow-up and closure to my search for the lives of those left behind — Rideout's wife and young family. However, despite a thorough examination of pertinent material, the names of other crew members with Captain Rideout could not be located.

4 *Murder and a Deathbed Confession*

Port au Port, Bonne Bay, Twillingate

An affair. Today these words carry a connotation of love and secret romance. The bold print in the newspaper read **The Rideout Affair** and the headline in the May 1877 *Harbour Grace Standard* caught my eye immediately. But in 1877 the word 'affair' had a different connotation. This affair hinted at murder and foul play on Newfoundland's west coast. The leak of a coverup and a dastardly deed of murder didn't come directly from investigators, from the victims' families, or from the perpetrators. The details of an alleged murder came from an unidentified third party — a man who confessed before he died.

The story **The Rideout Affair** (as presented by an unidentified informant from Bonne Bay) described the loss of Cap-

- **THE RIDOUT AFFAIR.**

A person from Bonne Bay yesterday gave the following respecting the loss of Captain Ridout and his crew. He inserts that his statement is only from hearsay, but he knew Mr. Ridout well. The gist of the statement is as follows:—

"Captain Ridout had £200 with him at the time he was supposed to be murdered. The craft went ashore close by a tilt occupied by an old hunter commonly known as "Jacko." All the

Newspapers of the day described the disappearance and possible murder of Captain Ridout (subsequently spelled Rideout) under the heading **The Rideout Affair**.

tain Fred Rideout and his crew. The word "loss" raised my curiosity immediately. A check of shipping registers and wreck lists shows that a vessel *Adonis* (often misidentified as *Grapeshot*), one of Duder's schooners, was wrecked on the west coast on December 20, 1874. Rideout and his crew left to walk to St. George's to get passage to St. John's, but were murdered en route. What really happened to Fred Rideout? What seamen sailed with him? Who committed the crime and why? From 1874 to 1877 the whereabouts or misfortunes of Rideout and his crew were not known and newspaper accounts were mysteriously silent.

Then, two and a half years after the wreck the fate of Captain Rideout and his men resurfaced. News of their deaths finally reached the St. John's papers. Why so long? Did distance or slow communication delay the telling of a dastardly deed? As the tale unravelled itself in May of 1877 with the headline "The Rideout Affair", the newspaper informant (who remained anonymous) said he knew Captain Rideout well and knew whereof he spoke; thus the final days of the captain and his men became clearer.

Adonis went ashore at Wild Cove, between Bay of Islands and Port au Port. The crew of seven reached shore safely and

Stranded on a barren and desolate land, an unidentified wreck lies grounded off shore. It was under such conditions, miles from a large town or shipping port, that Captain Fred Rideout and his crew were shipwrecked in *Adonis*.

built a rough shelter or erected a tent, probably from sail salvaged from the wreck. Captain Rideout's main concern was surviving December's winds and cold on a remote shore and finding a way to get back to St. John's. He had money — two or three hundred pounds — with him and that would help buy provisions, hire a guide or pay for transportation. *Adonis'* men soon realized they were miles from any town or port frequented by larger ships. Not far away from the campsite was a rough tilt or shack occupied by an old hunter who went by the name of "Jacko." Apparently Jacko, who was too old to guide the stranded men, gave directions for Channel/Port aux Basques where schooners sailing eastward for St. John's often stopped.

Rideout and his crew camped for a day or so north of Fox Island River, Port au Port Bay, perhaps getting the lay of the land. They were preparing themselves for a long journey by foot when a man, identified in daily newspapers as Gil Ben Waugh (Benoit) appeared at Rideout's campsite. Gil Benoit and his two brothers, Francis and Zavier, were hunters and wrackers — those who search for shipwrecks and salvage cargo from stranded ships.

21

Gil Benoit, who emerged as the leader of this brotherly group of desperados, visited the castaways at their tent and offered to guide them to Channel. With money to pay for such a favour, Rideout and his men gladly and blindly (as it turned out) accepted the offer. The castaways and would-be rescuers set out overland across the snow and frozen ponds. But Benoit had other plans and salvation was not one of them. While the group crossed an ice-covered pond, the crew of *Adonis* was murdered, shot in the back without a chance to defend themselves. Three of the seven fell on the first volley; the rest required another shot or two. The murderers cut a hole in the pond ice, robbed all money and useful clothes from the victims and put the bodies down in the pond.

But there were two who heard about the deed: Old Jacko and Gil Benoit's daughter, Agnes. Jacko knew the Rideout crew had gone with the would-be rescuers and had probably heard the shots ring out. Benoit and his brothers went back to Jacko offering money for complete silence. And silent Jacko was for two and a half years until he fell sick. Sickness and visions of heaven and hell played on Jacko's mind; he wished to confess. Soon Jacko's story with its rumours of foul play drifted back to St. John's. Jacko's confession brought to light the murder of Rideout and his crew. Once word of the foul play leaked out, the Newfoundland government asked Captain Erskine of the HMS *Eclipse*, a Nova Scotian-based vessel moored in Channel, to locate and hold any suspects and witnesses. Using the large cutter from *Eclipse* Erskine reached St. George's Bay and rounded up Gil, Francis and Zavier Benoit. They, along with witness Agnes Benoit, were to be brought to St. John's for trial. At first Gil Benoit went into hiding, but eventually was captured and brought to St. John's with the others.

The second person who knew about the murder was Agnes, then around eighteen years old. She had much to say about her father, Gil. Indeed if her story could be believed, she was the star witness. According to Agnes, her father was more of a monster than a man. Some of his deeds, according to the daily papers, were too repugnant to print. Agnes had heard him tell her grandmother he had shot three or four of Rideout's men. As a result of overhearing this conversation she had suffered several cruel beatings from her father, had twice been wounded in the head by a knife. He had threatened her life several times. On one occasion he chased her with a gun and she had only escaped by running into a river too deep for him to follow. Agnes would have drowned but her petticoats kept her afloat and she drifted downstream away from her enraged father. From that point on she lived away from home, thinking she would be killed upon return.

Agnes claimed that her uncles, Francis and Zavier, had seen blood-covered bodies from the wreck. Her father and her uncles had been away from home for several days about the time of the wreck and had taken their guns with them. They later returned laden with flour, clothes and other items from a wreck. Agnes was quick to add that her uncles did not touch the dead bodies for fear of being implicated in the crime.

Agnes had not actually seen any foul play; her version was based on circumstantial evidence and hearsay. Her motive for incriminating her father may have stemmed from ill-feelings toward him. Nevertheless authorities in St. John's believed the three Benoit men were guilty and had Captain Erskine hold them as suspects aboard the *Eclipse* at Channel. When the St. John's based steamer *Curlew*, Captain Jackman, arrived at Channel on her regular south coast run, the Benoits were transferred in irons to this ship and taken to St. John's.

S.S. *Curlew* arrived at two A.M. on Sunday, September 23, according to the September 25, 1877, edition of the newspaper *Ledger*. Despite the late hour several curious people went in quiet awe to the waterfront to view the murder suspects. The arrival of police inspector Lilly and those in custody was reported as:

Mr. Lilly returned by the S.S. *Curlew* on Sunday morning last, having been engaged by Government in eliciting evidence in the Rideout murder case. Gil Benoit and his brothers, Francis and Zavier, came by the *Curlew* and on

23

landing about two am, were escorted to the lockup by a posse of police, and a few ladies and gentlemen, who had risen from their slumbers to take a quiet look at the notorious Gil. The prisoners will be brought up before the Magistrate today on a hearing.

Hoping to find more witnesses and solid evidence, Inspector Carty with Sergeants Nichol and Sullivan sailed for the West Coast on October 14, 1877. Somewhat chagrined and disappointed, they returned in November without solving the crime, having failed to untangle the web of lies, half-truths, and deceit rampant in the Benoit family stories.

By the time of Benoit's arrest Old Jacko had probably died, but his stories hinted at other foul play by Benoit. Apparently a Nova Scotia fishing craft had been found on the shore some years prior to the Rideout murders. A Captain Sterling, his body partially decomposed and half-buried under a large rock, had been chopped to death. The axe that in all likelihood had killed him was by his side. People in the general area believed Sterling and his crew had been murdered by the same gang. The informant of Rideout's story was of the opinion that if HMS *Eclipse* were to sail to Port au Port or the general area the instances of murder and shipwracking would stop.

Hoping to find details of Benoit's trial or a satisfactory conclusion to the investigation, I searched other newspapers, especially the *Harbour Grace Standard* which carried the original story. Little could be found. The strange case of "The Rideout Murders" winds down when on December 1, 1877, when the St. John's papers reported that the Benoit brothers were released from prison. There would be no trial. The lack of evidence and unreliable witnesses couldn't substantiate the charge of murder in the deaths of Fred Rideout and his six men. In November, just prior to release, the youngest Benoit brother passed away in prison.

An unsatisfactory end to a dastardly crime? Could parts of this tale be the figment of someone's imagination or is it another gruesome murder mystery? Or did someone else commit a crime — old Jacko, maybe? Yet shipping lists and brief articles in newspapers confirm that the tale of murder, mayhem and confession on Newfoundland's west coast is true; albeit several key details of the story have since passed into legend and the complete truth may never be known.

The untimely death of Fred Rideout was passed down through Rideout family circles. Elizabeth Bursey of St. Philip's, a Rideout descendant, remembered the stories of her grandfather (Captain Fred Rideout's nephew) and recalled fleeting sketches of family tales — tales of shipwreck and murder. Fred Rideout was originally from the Twillingate area and lived in Back Harbour (Davis Cove). According to local history Rideout fishermen were the first to settle in Back Harbour.

Fred Rideout married Mary Clarke from Batrix Island, Twillingate, and they had six children. After the death of her husband, Mary relocated to St. John's with her young family who, at the time of the move, ranged in age from four to fourteen. She worked as a seamstress. Sometime in the 1880s Mary Rideout had saved enough money to move with her children to Boston. Two daughters, Lucy and Lillah, became nurses and were the first Newfoundlanders to graduate from the Massachusetts General Hospital School of Nursing. Lillah decided to further her career, went to medical school, and became a doctor and psychiatrist at the State Hospital in Pennsylvania. During World War One she served overseas with the Red Cross.

Son George Rideout became a Methodist minister with a doctorate in theology, preached all over the world and wrote many books on a variety of religious topics. William Rideout, who graduated from Harvard and later taught there, died early at age thirty-five. John Rideout graduated from and taught at Oxford University, England. A daughter, Lena, married Captain Edwin Giles of Greenspond. He commanded United States Fruit Company and Grace Line ships and voyaged extensively to the west coast of South America.

In the days of sail the schooner could be found in nearly every Newfoundland harbour. Because of their versatility, large numbers and general distribution, schooners appear in all sorts of unusual and stirring experiences, many of which became the subject of Newfoundland folk songs, poems and distinctive stories.

As I entered my early teens and frequented the Grand Bank waterfront, the schooner era was ending. Old workhorses like the *L.A. Dunton*, *Nina W. Corkum* and *Pauline C. Winters* often were tied up for months on end and, if used at all, were debased to coal carriers. As boys we trod their decks, climbed rigging and swung from cargo lifting ropes and hooks. Little did we realize it was the end of an age as one by one they slipped out between the western pier and the lighthouse never to return. Of a fleet of over three hundred vessels owned in Grand Bank over a period of one hundred years, the banker *L.A. Dunton*, a tourist attraction in Mystic, Connecticut, is one of only a few Newfoundland schooners still afloat.

Story five follows the career of the durable *Ornate*: built in Nova Scotia, she was used as a banking schooner in Fortune Bay, became a Labrador fishery schooner, and eventually ended her career in the coasting trade in Bonavista Bay.

5   One of the Unlucky Ones
St. Bernard's, Fair Island, Centreville, Farmyards, Lab

Nineteen twenty-eight was a year of trial and tribulation for the schooner *Ornate*. Trouble began on March 1 when *Ornate* left Fortune Bay for the fishing grounds. Owned by J.F. Parrott and Sons of St. Bernard's, Fortune Bay, *Ornate* carried twenty-three men and ten dories. The seventy-nine ton schooner had been built at Shelburne in 1913 and sold to Daniel Boyce of Jersey Harbour before Parrott's bought her.

Captain Parmenias "Men" Banfield of Bay L'Argent and mate James Cox of St. Bernard's didn't get the dories off deck for twenty days — this was totally unexpected. But exceptionally strong winds and stormy weather on the Western Bank fishing ground kept the men from setting trawls. Hugh Scott of St. Bernard's, a dory fisherman on *Ornate* that year, wrote down his experiences, saying:

> After nearly three weeks at sea we had to come into St. Pierre for water and then return to the Western Banks. We fished three baitings and caught 300 quintals or about 33,000 pounds. This ended the spring trip using frozen herring for bait.
>
> The first of June we fitted again for the capelin trip and July 2 we were fishing in the Straits when a storm came up. We lost two of our men through the swamping of their dory — Charlie Hayes of Parker's Cove, Placentia Bay, and mate James Cox.

As Scott remembered the trip, this turn of events, storms and the death of two shipmates whose bodies were not recovered, left a gloom over all the crew. Under very trying circumstances they managed to finish the trip. *Ornate* arrived back in St. Bernard's the first week in August with one thousand quintals.

The crew then fitted up for the fall trip. Captain Banfield, realizing it was too early to sail to the Labrador, said they would fish a small baiting on the Western Banks before going to the Labrador coast. That "small baiting" was an experience Hugh Scott vividly recalled:

> We left Rencontre West on Newfoundland's south coast on August 18 and the next day there was thick fog. The skipper planned to set out the fishing gear while under sail about one o'clock in the afternoon. While the dories fished in the morning, it became calm and the schooner drifted with the tide. Seven dories located the schooner, but the other three didn't make it.
>
> I was in one of the unlucky dories that didn't find the schooner. We were left stranded in the dories with no food at all and only one quart of water for six men.

Scott recalled the names of the other five men who were adrift with him on the open ocean in fog: George Vardy of Harbour Mille; Neil Banfield, Bay L'Argent; John James Brushett and his son, John Joe, of Jacques Fontaine; and George Cox, Terrenceville. He remembered:

> The first day we were astray we decided to let one dory go and put three men in each of the remaining two dories. This enabled us to row faster and provided more company for each other. As it turned out two hours after we let the dory adrift, our schooner *Ornate* picked it up, but we didn't know that at the time.
>
> We were in the dories three days and three nights with no food and little water for the six of us before we were picked up by a French banker on the St. Pierre Bank. We were on the French boat for five days when the schooner *Irene Corkum* from Grand Bank took us on board and brought us to St. Pierre.
>
> At St. Pierre we joined our own schooner *Ornate* and went to the Labrador to finish the trip. We arrived back home in St. Bernard's the first week in October with eleven hundred quintals for the voyage and shared $525 per man. This was considered a good paying voyage in those days.

Here Hugh Scott of St. Bernard's ends his account of the 1928 fishing season, one dotted with storm, hardship and the loss of men he knew well. As a seaman and breadwinner for his family he concluded with optimism and the knowledge that bank fishery had given him a "good paying voyage" in the end.

Two years later the Parrott business sold *Ornate*. She was taken to St. John's where, in the spring of 1930, John K. Rogers and his cousin Charles Rogers of Fair Island, Bonavista Bay, purchased the banker. The Rogers had lost their schooner *Janie Blackwood* when she was abandoned at sea one hundred and twenty miles off Newfoundland on December 12, 1929.

That first summer *Ornate*, skippered by Charles Rogers, plied the productive waters off the Labrador at Northern Island of Farmyards, north of Hopedale. While fishing there

In the spring of 1930, when Captain Charles Rogers, his cousin John and three crewmen, Israel Rogers, Frederick Hounsell and Hedley Brown, went from Fair Island to St. John's to buy and bring *Ornate* (above) home, they travelled there in an open motorboat — a feat of seamanship in itself. On the way back, the towrope to the motorboat broke and the small boat was lost.

The fishing town of Fair Island has been abandoned since the 1960s, but former residents, like Alan Rogers who supplied much basic information for *Ornate*'s story, return to reminisce and to fish.

a heavy ground swell rose up unexpectedly, destroyed all of *Ornate*'s codtraps, and totally wrecked the *Nanchu*, a schooner owned by Jabez Winsor of Wesleyville. The crew was able to reach land on the Farmyards safely. Another schooner, *James U. Thomas* captained by James Carter of Greenspond, was anchored near the islands and was not damaged. *Ornate*'s crew knew the shipwrecked men were all accounted for on the Farmyards and the next day carried them to Hopedale to connect with transportation home to Newfoundland.

However two of *Nanchu*'s crew, Israel Ackerman and Ephriam Rogers, asked the two co-owners of *Ornate* if they could come aboard the schooner for the remainder of the summer. Charles and John Rogers consented, for *Ornate* at this time was three quarters loaded and the two men would help secure a full load. With *Ornate*'s traps gone, they had to

Photo courtesy of Alan Rogers, Centreville

In the late fall of 1945 *Ornate* was pulled up at Fair Island for extensive repairs. Her tonnage increased from ninety-six to one hundred eleven ton. Throughout the years of the Labrador fishery, Charles and John Rogers also owned *Ben Hur* and *Camperdown*. When *Ornate* was lost the Rogers purchased the schooner *National Convention* which they renamed *Dorothy Marie II* after their daughters.

In 1967 they built *Prudence Ann* and used her for four years. This vessel was sold and may have eventually ended up in St. Pierre.

rely on jiggers to fish. At Double Islands, nine miles inside of Farmyards, they jigged enough cod to make a paying voyage, so important to two shipwrecked breadwinners of Wesleyville.

From her home base at Fair Island, *Ornate* engaged in the Labrador fishery each summer from 1930 to 1950 and brought supplies from St. John's to Bonavista Bay in the spring and fall.

Workhorses like *Ornate* not only contributed to the economic viability and well-being of Bonavista Bay islands, but also knitted into the social fabric of the people themselves. The Rogers' schooners, like all vessels of the islands, became a home away from home for many travellers. Whenever *Ornate* went to St. John's there were always passengers going on her. Others who had gone to St. John's by train could, if they wished, stay aboard the schooner if she was tied up there. No thought was ever given to charge for transportation or lodging.

Lester, the son of Captain Charles Rogers, recalls that at one point during World War Two there was a railway strike and *Ornate* left St. John's with thirty-seven passengers and crew aboard. During the voyage northward, they encountered a thick fog, but arrived in Fair Island safely. Had there been an accident the people would have had to depend on two small boats which served as lifeboats on *Ornate*.

Beginning in 1950, due in part to a downturn in the markets for salt fish, *Ornate* followed only the coasting trade. Her final hours came on April 26, 1959, while en route from St. John's to Bonavista Bay and fully laden with general cargo. Nine miles off Grates Point, Trinity Bay, she met with Arctic ice, steamed through it, but sprang a leak in the log shaft. The M.V. *Glenwood* took *Ornate* in tow, but the old faithful schooner slowly sank. Her crew — Captain Lester Rogers, his brother and mate Ronald Rogers, Charles Rogers, Marshall Brown and engineer Gilbert Pickett all of Fair Island — watched her give a final nod of farewell.

It started when the telephone rang on August 9, 1998. Of all the people Dorothy Kavanagh could have contacted in Newfoundland to begin this epic of the *Florence* she chose me. I'm grateful, but amazed and mystified by chain of coincidences. Dorothy saw my name as a shipwreck contact in an *Elderhostel* magazine, found my phone number and called to ask if I knew anything of the wreck of the brig *Florence* in 1840. I didn't.

During the winter of 1998-99, she sent me her family's anecdotal information while I searched other sources for details on the wreck. As the story grew and I learned of the plight of the survivors of *Florence*, I could imagine the band of German immigrants struggling along the cliffs and paths from Cape Race to Renews. Dorothy Kavanagh (and the image of a rag-tag group of survivors) re-kindled a spark of Newfoundland history and lit a cosy fire under this account.

In early July 1999, I sent the story to the *Evening Telegram* and on August 1 it appeared in print (few days before the 159th anniversary of the shipwreck). When the descendants of *Florence*'s survivors visited the Southern Shore and the wreck scene, CBC television recorded the event. As well Chris Brookes audio-taped portions and his production of "Great, Great, Greats: The Wreck of the *Florence*" aired internationally some months later. "Full Circle" is my version of how the story grew.

6 *Full Circle: The Wreck of Florence, 1840*

Renews, Cape Race

hat is the inner force or drive which compels a writer to tell the tale? The late Cassie Brown, when commenting on her writing of the book *Death on the Ice*, said, "I sensed a force, a hand reach down to hold my wrist. I knew then I had to finish the story." Seventy-eight sealers who died on the Arctic ice in March, 1914 had no chance to tell of their horrific ordeal, but Brown, who talked of a need, an urge to complete her book, told their story eloquently in her 1972 epic of sealing and suffering.

Fifteen hundred kilometres away in Hartford, Connecticut, Dorothy Kavanagh reached out to contact Newfoundland, particularly the people of Renews and St. John's. She knew no one in Newfoundland, but an inner voice or gut-feeling convinced her someone would help and a connection would be made. I received a call from Dorothy, who asked if I had information on the wreck of *Florence*, a brig that came to an untimely end near Cape Race in 1840 with loss of fifty lives.*

A direct descendant of a survivor of the wreck of *Florence*, Dorothy felt she needed to know more of the town of Renews and St. John's, whose residents long ago aided and sheltered those who escaped drowning. She wanted to learn about the geography, the people and the ways of Newfoundland. Thus began a correspondence which culminated August 9th, 1999 when Dorothy, her brother Alfred and other family members visited Newfoundland and the area where their ancestors landed long ago.

One source of information about the wreck of *Florence* comes from the September 3, 1840, issue of the New York newspaper *New Era*, a copy of which had been collected by Dorothy's sister Mary, the family historian. This evidence supports Mary's longstanding anecdotal history. *New Era's* heading hinted at the extent of the calamity and the text detailed an all-too-familiar story of disaster:

Awful Wreck

Brig *Attention* arrived here (New York) yesterday from St. John's, N.F. with the melancholy recital of the loss of the brig *Florence* and fifty lives. The particulars were furnished to Capt. McCurdy by some person on board the lost brig and are therefore entirely correct.

---

* Later I asked her how and why she found my name. It was in an Elderhostel catalogue which describes various studies one can do in North America.

The following disaster is one of those awful occurrences with which the South Eastern coast of Newfoundland is often the scene. The brig *Florence* and from New York, Captain Samuel Rose, sailed from Rotterdam, June 30, 1840 with a crew of eight persons and seventy-nine passengers, cargo, ballast and a few casks of wine.

They were with pleasant weather until nearly up with the eastern part of the Banks of Newfoundland when they were assaulted with a succession of gales, attended with fog and rain up to the time of their shipwreck.

On Sunday morning August 9 the man on the lookout cried "hard down the helm, breakers ahead." The helm was immediately put-a-lee, but before the sails were taken aback the brig struck the rocks on her starboard side.

She instantly filled and fell over on her side, when a scene of confusion and terror presented itself, the horror of which can better be imagined than described. Here were the wife and husband bidding each other a last farewell, the frantic mother clasping her infant to her bosom as if death itself should not separate them; while some few who had relatives on board were endeavouring to secure what money they had, by fastening it to their bodies, but which alas proved the means of their destruction; for that which they vainly thought would secure to them a comfortable home in the fertile lands of the far "West" changed their destination to an eternal home in death. On attempting to swim to the land the weight of the money sank them to the bottom.

Captain Rose with commendable coolness commanded all to remain by the wreck until some means were devised for escaping with safety.

For this purpose Mr. William Robbs of Springfield, Massachusetts took the end of a line and sprang from the vessel to a ledge which lay between her and the shore. An overwhelming wave however, overtook the devoted sailor and dashed him against the rocks, a mangled corpse.

Rose next attempted this, the only means of gaining the land in safety. The crew was all saved except the second mate. But only thirty of the seventy-nine passengers were saved and of these many were saved by Capt. Rose and Chief Mate Scofield at the imminent peril of their own lives.

By the time these were saved about three hours after the brig struck there were scarcely two of her planks together, all were literally in splinters.

Thus thirty-seven persons were thrown ashore in a barren land on an unknown part of the coast. Many of them were but half clad and most of them were without shoes. Not a solitary biscuit was saved. In this pitiable condition they commenced their journey through thick woods and swamps and over bleak and rugged hills in hopes of finding some human habitation.

For four days they continued their course, governed chiefly by the wind; the sun, moon and stars being obscured nearly all the time by fog and rain and squalls which later were very frequent — sometimes eating berries they could find. Early on the morning of the 13th, Capt. Rose and Scofield ascended a hill in hopes the fog might clear off and afford them a view of the surrounding country. At nine o'clock the weather cleared a little and they were enabled to see the harbour and village of Renouse (Renews). The happy information was soon communicated to the rest and they resumed their march with lighter hearts.

When they entered the village, its hospitable inhabitants welcomed them with everything which their present needs demanded. Mr. Goodridge of whose benevolence the crew and passengers speak in the warmer terms of gratitude, gave money and clothes to them; then furnished a vessel to convey them to St. John's, the residence of the U.S. Consular agent.

At seven P.M. on Saturday the 15th, they were landed at St. John's. The news of their arrival soon brought to the shore rich and poor, old and young some thrusting bread into the hands of the shipwrecked strangers and others taking the poor wretches home with them.

Nothing was spared to alleviate their wants and sufferings. The next day being Sunday nothing was publicly done for them. A notice was posted on the billboards requesting a meeting to take place at the Chamber of Commerce of the U.S. to devise means to relieve the necessities of those whom fate had thrown upon their shores. Some 70 or 80 pounds were collected in a short time, and resolutions were passed to raise a sufficient sum whereby

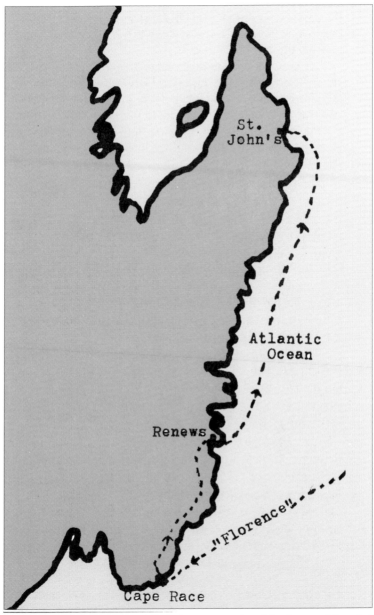

In the five day trek northward, it is likely the castaways kept inland on a well-travelled trail or path. Thus they avoided long indraughts or coastal cliffs and skirted heavy undergrowth or trees near the shoreline. In the fog they probably didn't see other smaller towns scattered along the coast until they reached Renews.

the emigrants might be enabled to reach the place of their destination.

A committee was appointed to receive clothing and money from all who felt disposed to give.

We believe the *Florence* was nearly a new vessel. She sailed from this port (New York) last spring for Rotterdam and was on her return voyage here.

With only half the passengers surviving, no doubt there were terrible stories of tragedy on that August day and just as likely, great feats of heroism. Details of exactly what transpired are now lost in the mists of time.

Dorothy Kavanagh's great grandfather was Michael J. Adrian who was thirteen years old when the *Florence* was wrecked. He was carried safely ashore on his father's shoulders on the breeches buoy rigged up by Captain Rose and Mate Scofield. Michael's brother Stephen, about eighteen years of age, also made it safely ashore.

Their parents, Gertrude and Johannes Pieter (Peter) Adrian, who both survived the wreck, came to North America with their children from Klingenberg, Bavaria. A relative aunt "pulled her skirts over her head" and jumped in panic to certain death.

"This was the way my grandmother, Mary Adrian the daughter of Michael, told the story," Dorothy recalled. "And I remember her speculating that her forebears, Gertrude and Peter, were coming to the United States to avoid military service for their sons. They were not young. Gertrude was in her late forties. What courage they had."

To help Dorothy with her quest, I searched the St. John's newspaper *Public Ledger*. In the Tuesday, August 18, 1840, edition under the heading **Melancholy Shipwreck** it was reported that:

The two hundred ton *Florence* struck about one mile west of Cape Race on August 9. From the time the survivors landed near Cape Race to the evening of the 13th, when they reached Renews (without any guide), they had subsisted wholly on berries, no one in the neighbourhood having been aware of the catastrophe which had taken place.

The correspondent at Renews, in speaking to the *Public Ledger*, claimed that no case of shipwreck in this country that had come within his knowledge, had "been more entitled to sympathy, or in which assistance has been more required."

Judge Robert Carter, stationed on the southern shore in the 1800s, kept a diary (from 1832 to 1852) and recorded newsworthy events. Much of his diary was published in a local paper in 1927. His August 18, 1840 entry reads:

> Accounts reached here from Renews that the part of the crew and passengers of a vessel from Amsterdam for New York reached this place having come from Cripple Cove, near Cape Race, on foot. It is said that 50 are drowned and 30 passengers saved. The latter taken to St. John's today in a boat from Renews.

At that time, the southern shore town had a population of around six hundred and its residents shared what they had. Alan Goodridge and Sons, the principal mercantile business in Renews, provided the survivors with transportation by sea to St. John's. When the thirty-seven refugees who had been suddenly thrust upon the city arrived on Saturday evening of August 15th, 1840 the general public, like the good citizens of Renews, reached out to help. The greatest concern was to properly clothe, feed and house the survivors. Then, once those needs had been assured, funds for transportation to New York would be raised.

On Monday August 17th, the president of the St. John's Chamber of Commerce posted a notice requesting a meeting at the Commercial Room at two P.M. Within hours, a subscription list for donations opened and contributions came in.

A committee was appointed for the purpose of collecting further monies and within a day £62 had been raised. Another charitable group in St. John's in the mid-1800s was the Ladies of the Dorcas Society, a women's organization whose

One of three ads which appeared in the St. John's paper *Public Ledger* in August 1840 concerning the survivors of the wrecked *Florence*. The above solicits a ship.

chief aim was to provide clothes for the needy. They immediately distributed clothing to the survivors of the *Florence*.

The "Florence Subscription List" Committee members were Chairman William Thomas (the Honourable Attorney General), Messrs. Scott, Grieve, Bulley, S. Mudge, Robert Prowse, Thomas Job and John Trimingham. William Thomas and Thomas Job agreed to take care of any clothing collected while others had the responsibility of finding transportation to New York. Within a few days a vessel left St. John's for New York with *Florence*'s thirty passengers and seven crew aboard.

The Adrians, like the other survivors, arrived in New York penniless, having lost their possessions in the wreck. Michael, however, reversed his fortunes. Eventually he became a landowner in New York, founded the German Exchange Bank which later merged with and became a branch of the First National City Bank of New York. Michael Adrian had six children whose progeny are now scattered across the United States and abroad. In August 1999, several descendants of Gertrude, Peter and Michael Adrian made a pilgrim-

Courtesy Adrian Kavanagh

Cape Race (A) and Cripple Cove. Brig *Florence* was wrecked on the rugged cliffs stretching behind Coleen Kavanagh, a descendant of a *Florence* survivor.

age to the shores of Newfoundland to view the shipwreck area and to thank the towns which aided their forbearers many years ago. Today part of the East Coast Hiking Trail which extends from Cape Race to St. John's commemorates the arduous trek of *Florence* survivors.

As for Renews, located eighty-three kilometres south of St. John's, it was not the first time immigrants from across the Atlantic had stopped at the picturesque town. It was settled in the sixteenth century by migratory seasonal fishermen, then by English/Irish colonists and planters. The *Newfound-*

land Encyclopedia claims (although there are many who refute the claim) the ship *Mayflower*, while bringing the Pilgrims from Plymouth, England to America in 1620 stopped at Renews for supplies.

Perhaps the story of visitation, shipwreck, and goodwill is intertwined in the cyclical nature of the ocean forever pounding on Newfoundland's doorstep. Maybe that's what compels all of us to search for some sense of satisfactory closure to another epic of the sea.

Often in tales describing shipwreck on Newfoundland's coast, the hint of illegal activities surfaces — suggestions that "Wrackers lured the ship ashore" or "The person tied a lantern on the cow's horns and the ship's crew, thinking the light came from a lighthouse, steered a course which put them aground."

Many tales of wrackers have now reached the level of legend where truth and fiction are merged. I have read of or researched hundreds of wrecks and have seen very little to substantiate deliberate luring ships ashore or "wracking." Very few folk tales of our island tell of wrackers brought to justice. This story relates the opposite — the generous spirit of Newfoundland pioneers who helped when ships and lives were in jeopardy. Only in extreme measures, as hinted at the conclusion of their story, would anyone intentionally lure a ship ashore.

7   *Derelict Ship, Disgruntled Salvors*

Bay Bulls, St. John's

In February 1881, the Newfoundland Vice-Admiralty Court decided on a salvage settlement for the derelict ship *Alice Lyne*. The men who had submitted a monetary claim under British salvage laws were from Bay Bulls. The names of the twenty-one claimants are listed at the conclusion of this chapter. Although details of ownership, size or the cause of the stranding of *Alice Lyne* have not been recorded, it is known *Alice Lyne* lived to sail again; not a common phenomenon for ships stranded on the unfriendly rocks along our island shores.

Sometime in late January 1881 *Alice Lyne* grounded five miles north of Bay Bulls. Her crew took to a single lifeboat, rowed into Bay Bulls, and proclaimed the ship an abandoned derelict. The weather that day was terrible, for a North Atlantic storm had brought high winds, freezing temperatures and snow. Combers and white surf pounded the Avalon Peninsula's southern shore.

Had there been a telegraph station in Bay Bulls the operator would have immediately contacted authorities in St. John's to inform them of the wreck. But a line had not yet been extended to the Avalon southern shore and for residents along the shore it became a case of act first, ask questions later.

When vessels are unlucky enough to strike the reefs off Newfoundland and Labrador's rocky shoreline, landsmen in the area do what they can to save lives. That becomes their primary concern. But when human lives are not in danger, people swarm to the crippled, stranded vessel making good use of spoils of the sea.

When a ship is abandoned, these looters, termed 'wrackers', usually take whatever can be lifted and carried away — food, ship's fittings, sails, gear, equipment, and articles of cargo become especially desirable. Wood, if of no immediate use, could be stored for home fires later. Traditionally, many wrackers operated within the legal boundaries, acted with permission, or reported their bounty, but others disregarded the law, taking what they could despite the captain's warnings.

When the Bay Bulls men reached the derelict *Alice Lyne* they acted legally, thus, were salvors — not "ship wrackers" — and were entitled to full salvage benefits under marine law.

To reach the abandoned wreck required a feat bordering on heroism. Of eight hundred people living near the wreck site, only twenty-one volunteered to brave the elements. After rowing five miles in small open boats, through heavy seas and bailing water constantly, they located the vessel. *Alice Lyne* had drifted off the outermost reef and lay a few hundred feet from breakers near shore.

Not knowing when she would strike rocks or become unmanageable in the high winds, the Bay Bulls men boarded *Alice Lyne* and slowly but successfully kept her away from shore. If they had been one hour later she would have smashed on the jagged rocks. But as it turned out, the ship sailed into St. John's intact. Salvors took great care and delivered her to the Admiralty Court with not even, as they described it, a ropeyarn or line injured or broken.

An editorial in the city paper dated February 21, 1881, stated that "while the Bay Bulls men had possession of the vessel the greatest care was taken of everything about her." The valiant salvors themselves said, "We destroyed nothing on board of her, but brought her in as we found her. The whole affair was attended with the greatest peril and risk of life."

They knew the sum of the whole was worth more than its parts. Ship and cargo intact was valued at £ 5,500 (about $15,000 in today's values) — a deal much better than any paltry gains made from "wracking" or destroying the ship and contents. Salvage laws would award them one quarter value, around £1300.

Then the verdict came down. To the chagrin and vocal consternation of the twenty-one claimants, the Court of Vice-Admiralty deemed *Alice Lyne* worth £3,500 and gave the group the paltry sum of £625 to be shared between them. Subtracted from this sum were towing costs and court expenses. They were forced to settle for a little over twenty-two pounds each or $55.00.

The Bay Bulls' men voiced their disbelief and dismay to the local papers: "Had we not acted legally in a time when Newfoundland people were branded wrackers by the Whiteway-Shea government?" They also claimed that several fishermen, just for taking a few fathom of rope for remuneration for services rendered, had been brought to St. John's, tried, and jailed. Would Newfoundlanders, in the future, refuse to lend a willing hand unless paid first?

It is not known if their protest changed anything or if they carried through with implied threats, but in a harsh letter to the February 25 *Evening Telegram*, the twenty-one Bay Bulls fishermen concluded, "We intend, if fortune may cast another vessel on our shores, to treat her in a far different manner." The letter was appended (with spelling and duplication as the signatures appeared in the paper) by:

Richard Mokeler	John Williams	Michael Brien
Patrick Williams	Cornelius Brien	Ambrose Williams
Michael Ryan	Michael Williams	Edward Williams
Joseph Williams	Cornelius Brien	Thos. Getherell
Brien O'Brien	John Getherell	James Glinn
William Gatherell	Martin Brien	Michael Williams
Joseph Williams	William Driscoll	William Getherell

Courtesy Yvonne Andrieux

The bones of an ancient wreck. *Alice Lyne* was salvaged by the men of Bay Bulls before she ended up a buried derelict.

It has been recorded that over ten thousand ships have met their end along Newfoundland's rugged coastline, over 6000 miles long. Most of these wrecks happened within a time span of one hundred years, roughly defined as 1850 to 1950 when the era of sail and schooner came and went.

During those years the schooner was an important and vital transportation link along Newfoundland's shores. The maritime records are full of stories in which schooners — the small coasters and fish collectors, the six to twelve dory bankers and the larger foreign going terns — and their crews played an essential role. Self-sacrifice, daring, skill, wreck, and rescue are all part of a fabric which makes up the history of the schooner and the heritage of the towns that knew them. Many people in Newfoundland remember the stories and wish to share them with others. Chapter eight has two such accounts.

In January 1999 I spoke on "Cross Talk," a CBC St. John's radio program. People with an interest in the sea and ships called in and we talked. One woman asked about her father's ship wrecked many years ago. I took a note of the date and later searched for confirmation or extra information. The story of *Emily E. Selig* is the result.

The second tale of a ship comes from Garry Forward of Tizzard's Harbour and was subsequently verified by the *Evening Telegram* of November 1, 1892, as well as an article in the *Twillingate Sun* of November 12, 1892.

8 The Tale of Two Ships
Tizzard's Harbour, Flower's Cove, Grey Islands

A shipwreck story told in Newfoundland kitchens had a theme all too familiar: a schooner's was crew stranded on a desolate island and survived for days on what little food the immediate land could provide. Finally, the castaways were located and rescued. This was plight of the crew of *Emily E.*

Selig in November 1927 and, although her story is brief, it deserves to be recorded.

On November 10, 1927, schooner wreckage was seen on the eastern side of the Great Northern Peninsula which supposedly had drifted from the Grey Islands. One vessel posted overdue that November was the *Emily E. Selig* and the wreckage was presumably from this schooner. The *Daily News* of November 14 reprinted a message received from Magistrate Alcock of St. Anthony which stated, "Feared *Emily Selig* foundered with crew."

Built in 1915 at Lunenburg, Nova Scotia, *Emily E. Selig* eventually came under the ownership of J.A. George and Sons of Flower's Cove. She left St. John's on November 1, 1927, headed for her home port of Flower's Cove with a cargo of supplies for the long winter — flour, sugar, other staple food and shop goods — necessary for the survival of relatively isolated coastal towns. In command of *Selig* was Captain Walter Chaytor of Wesleyville/Greenspond. Only one other of her five or six crewmen is known: Nat Noel of Harbour Grace (the father of the CBC caller).

To reach Flower's Cove, located on the western side of the Great Northern Peninsula, *Selig* passed near the tip of the Great Northern Peninsula. Vessels bound northward from St. John's usually made the trip in three or four "legs" or overnight stops. One of her stops may have been St. Anthony or St. Julien's in which case she had to pass north of Grey Islands, two great granite blocks of islands located south of St. Anthony.

The north island is Grois Island, often called Northern Grey Island, 9.6 km (6 miles) long and 4 km (2.5 miles) broad at its widest part. The land is boldly marked by high cliffs and thickly wooded areas. Grois Island is fairly flat but can be seen from the sea on a clear day from a distance of eighty kilometres away.

It was upon this desolate coast the schooner *Emily E. Selig* stranded. Captain Chaytor, Nat Noel and the crew scrambled ashore in safety, but were cut off from the outside world. In the several days up to the time of rescue, they existed on partridgeberries, dried and frozen on the barren hills.

Eventually when another ship came by, they were seen and taken off the island. *Emily E. Selig*'s crew finally reached St. Anthony where the resident magistrate sent another message to St. John's saying the men were alive and well. *Daily News* November 14, 1927, carried the final words on the schooner:

> *Emily E. Selig*, Chaytor master, bound to Flower's Cove with supplies, lost on Northern Grey Island. Crew safe.

On November 19 *Selig*'s wreckage and cargo drifted south. Captain Johnson sailing in the schooner *Edward Johnson* reported passing through wreckage of the schooner near Grois Island.

Although *Selig*'s crew endured hardships, they survived. Many other seamen and ships fell prey to the ocean; their

Photo courtesy of Seamen's Museum

Emily E. Selig (above) wrecked at Grois Islands early November 1927. At one point in *Selig*'s career she was captained by John Barrett of Spaniard's Bay. Captain Walter Chaytor (1892-1933) of the *Selig* had previously been skipper of the *Maxwell R* and mate of *Hazel P. Blackwood*.

final fate and their attempt to reach safety were never documented. All we have is mute evidence of debris and wreckage cast ashore on lonely beaches and jagged rocks. Such was the case of a vessel out of Tizzard's Harbour, which like the *Emily E. Selig*, was employed in the coasting-trading run for fish and supplies. So it was with the schooner *Emeril* which sailed from Twillingate on October 2, 1892, for St. John's.

On the northward voyage home one of her intended stops was the fishing community of Seldom-Come-By, located on the southern shore of Fogo Island. In the era of sail Seldom-Come-By, a well-sheltered harbour north of Greenspond, became an important stopover port for vessels traversing Newfoundland's northern coastlines. A little to the west of Seldom, Stag Harbour Run was known as an especially tricky passage, not to be attempted unless conditions were favourable.

Emeril, owned jointly by J.B. Tobin and the Gates family of Tizzard's Harbour, was under the command of Robert Percy of Back Harbour, near Twillingate. John and James Gates of Tizzard's Harbour and William White of Ragged Point, made up the rest of the crew. Of the four, apparently only Percy had much experience on the coastal run. He had been to St. John's previously by boat and for that reason was given command of the schooner.

By November 5 news trickled into Twillingate and the surrounding communities that *Emeril* had been wrecked on Cann Island off Seldom-Come-By on October 29. Information came from other vessels that sailed from St. John's in company with the Gates' schooner. Seamen figured *Emeril* met her doom on the Brandies while sailing in a storm. A treacherous shoal of rocks, the Brandies lie eastward of Cann Island.

Other schooners sailing with *Emeril* ran under foresail and jib; one or two found it necessary to hoist the mainsail immediately after making Cann Island light. Since the wind had veered in the evening, the extra sail would help them steer away from the Brandies. The weather had changed to strong south and southwest wind and rain accompanied by

Photo courtesy Gary Forward, Tizzard's Harbour

Tizzard's Harbour before 1933 with Clothier Island to the left and the Orange Hall, the white building, centre. Today Clothier Island is vacant, but was once filled with homes, stages and sheds. The schooner moored in foreground is the *Allah Akbar*, owned by Joseph William Osmond. *Allah Akbar* was lost in November 1933.

heavy fog and heavy seas, making it impossible to see land even from a half mile away.

Emeril carried four crew. Veteran seamen could only speculate that was not enough manpower to get the mainsail up in time. Probably, since there were no survivors to tell the tale, they ran upon the breakers and shoals of the Brandies. Some debris and broken planks drifted near Seldom-Come-By the next morning.

Several identifying pieces of the wrecked schooner were picked up including a watch or clock which had stopped at seven o'clock. This was about the time other schooners saw, in the darkening skies, the ill-fated Tizzard's Harbour schooner trying to beat past the Brandies near Cann Island. William White, the son of James White of Ragged Point, was a widower but the other men — skipper Robert Percy of Back Harbour, John Gates, his brother James Gates — each left a wife and two or three children.

Tizzard's Harbour, a fishing town on New World Island,

Notre Dame Bay lies about six kilometres southwest of Twill-ingate. It was settled in the late 1790s or early 1800s and six fishing rooms were recorded there: those of John Bide (Boyd), John Forward, Andrew Locke, William Lacey, Philip Wiseman and Thomas Colbourne. The 1936 Census shows a population of nineteen families and one hundred twenty people. Today, despite resettlement and out-migration, its population is stable at about one hundred.

In the spring of 1999, when I first began to write and collect stories for *Raging Winds...Roaring Sea*, I intended to record only those terrible sea disasters of ships that had disappeared without a trace (such as the *Emeril* in the previous chapter). But along the way, I realized I also needed to preserve the heroic deeds of Newfoundland men and women who faced certain death on the ocean, but overcame the odds stacked against them and lived to tell the tale.

This is a Christmas sea story, not something usually associated with Newfoundland Christmases. This episode of adversity happened at a time when many people decorate, wrap presents, bake, and prepare for the festive season. But festivity was far from the minds of six Conception Bay seamen in December of 1904 as they fought bitter December winds and struggled to stay alive. Theirs is a story of ingenuity, endurance and ultimately of survival.

9   *Hardship on the Ocean*

Harbour Grace, Carbonear

*W*hen *Gladys* left Harbour Grace on a Monday morning of December 19th, 1904, the weather was fine, and a light breeze was blowing, just enough to push the topsail schooner along at a good clip. But winter conditions on the high seas can change dramatically, as the seamen soon discovered.

Gladys, owned by Duff and Balmer of Carbonear, had been built in North Wales in Williams' shipyard and had once carried the Welsh name of "Gwladys." Captain Reuben Pike, employed by Duff and Balmer for twenty-five years, had with him hardy veterans of the sea who hailed mostly from Carbonear or Harbour Grace: mate James McCarthy, bosun Michael Sweeney, cook John Babb, seamen Thomas Moore and Robert Hedge.

By one P.M. *Gladys* passed Cape St. Francis and straightened away for Bristol, England, where she was bound with a cargo of fish and oil. Sailing conditions remained much the same on Tuesday and Wednesday. By Thursday, December 22, the wind freshened accompanied by heavy snow. Captain Pike gave orders to shorten canvas. Deckhands Moore, Hedge, and Sweeney skipped to the top, stowed the upper topsail and double-reefed (or tied) the mizzen.

Weather worsened such that by December 24, Christmas Eve, the strong southeast gale forced nearly all the crew to labour at the sails: double-reef the mainsail, double-reef the mizzen again, foresail single-reefed, and by eight P.M. the lower topsail had to be taken in. At midnight the wind reached hurricane force, forcing Captain Pike to heave to.

The glass went "bottom up" as the saying goes, dropping to 28.10 and all aboard prepared for a rough night. Christmas Day was one long remembered by the crew: the wind veered to northwest and exceeded hurricane force, seas rose quickly. Deeply laden, *Gladys* took a pounding. Whitecaps constantly breached her deck, making it dangerous for the crew to move around.

At one P.M., a gigantic wave buried the ship, sending tons of water everywhere. Before the vessel recovered, a second wave breached the deck which threw *Gladys* on her beam ends. For several minutes she remained there — hatch combings in the water — and didn't come upright until the crew chopped away the mainsail.

When the ship came back on an even keel, Captain Pike viewed the tremendous damage inflicted. The mizzen sail which had been double reefed was gone, swept over the side; the water ways* were loosened; and the stanchions on the lee side were broken off. The latter literally "did the vessel in" as mate McCarthy stated later. He reported, "Immediately water began to pour down into the cabin and hold where the stanchions were broken."

However, they worked around the clock pumping, caulking leaks with brin bags and repairing damage inflicted by raging seas. All Christmas night the hurricane increased in

---

* Channels below the bulwarks designed to take water off deck.

strength and seas seethed in white foam and flying spray. The next day there was no change in the storm, but the six seamen were exhausted from the previous forty-eight hours of non-stop labour.

The evening of Boxing Day brought no respite; matters, if possible to imagine, deteriorated. Another sea swept the decks that virtually sent *Gladys* to the bottom. The two boats were torn from their lashings and battered to pieces, the galley was lifted from the iron fastenings that held it to the deck, the rails were torn away and the main and mizzen booms were broken. Everything moveable on deck was washed over the side.

Gladys now began to leak rapidly. While two men bailed water from the hold by buckets, Michael Sweeney and Thomas Moore were lashed to the two pumps. They were only pumping half an hour when another monster wave broke over the luckless craft. Sweeney and Moore suffered bruises and internal injuries. Sweeney, in particular, writhed in pain on the deck when he saw the cook John Babb going over the side. Babb was in the water a moment when the schooner lurched and miraculously he washed back near the broken rail again. Sweeney, in agony, grabbed and held on to Babb as he was passing overboard again.

Up to midnight December 26, these conditions continued without letup. Lashed to the pumps for hours while chilled to the bone from icy seas, became the lot of *Gladys'* crew, and this without a morsel of food or warm drink. On the 27th wind moderated, but relentless seas continued to send white combers across the decks. Water rose steadily in the hold and *Gladys* began to list, slightly at first, but more and more within a few hours.

By daylight that day Captain Pike knew his ship could not survive. He decided to run her before the storm under bare poles, or without sail, in order to get her on an even keel. To keep the mainboom from pounding the decks, he and mate McCarthy lashed it to a stanchion.

Another sea, described later as even higher than any previous, carried both captain and mate overboard.

McCarthy rose up on the swell, grasped the main rigging, and held on. Captain Pike was not so fortunate. He was carried over *Gladys'* stern. When seaman Hedge, who was at the wheel, saw what had happened he brought the ship about hoping to find the captain.

It was not to be. There were no boats aboard, and if there had been, it would have been suicide to launch one. Within a minute, Pike had drifted too far away to catch any objects his shipmates could throw into the high seas. The last they saw of their unfortunate captain, heavily clad but likely paralysed from near-freezing water, he was about a half mile away.

The saddened crew had to finally turn their ship away and attempt to keep it afloat a little longer. They attached a tarpaulin in the mizzen rigging, a storm sail on the mizzen boom and kept *Gladys* running before the wind. There was still no sleep for anyone; all pumped without letup.

The wind lessened on the morning of Wednesday, December 28 and mate McCarthy, now in command, took stock: "A heavy sea was running, the crew was near exhaustion, arms chaffed, hands swollen and ulcerated. But there was no giving in, nor complaining. We expected a sail (rescue ship) to heave in sight."

Indeed, at four P.M. they saw an eastbound steamer in the distance. A fire, or flare-up as *Gladys* crew termed it, was hoisted in the rigging. The men, worn to exhaustion in their battle, rejoiced; rescue was at hand. By dark the steamer was still in sight, the flare-ups still burned, but the steamer passed over the horizon. McCarthy claimed after it was impossible for the steamer not to see the signal.

During the long, lonely night two other steamers were seen, but they "paid not the slightest attention to our distress signals," said McCarthy. When daylight finally broke, the sun was a welcome sight although the loss of their captain and the passing of the ships had made the remaining five men desperate.

Daylight brought new trouble. The crew discovered four and half feet of water in the hold. With two men at the pumps, the other three jettisoned the cargo and this brought

RED - CROSS - LINE

Weekly Service of Passenger and Freight Steamers between

NEW YORK - HALIFAX, N.S.
AND
ST. JOHN'S, NEWFOUNDLAND

SPECIAL TOURIST CRUISES IN SUMMER

OLDEST
STEAMSHIP LINE
IN THE
NEWFOUNDLAND
TRADE

ONLY DIRECT
SERVICE BETWEEN
NEWFOUNDLAND
AND
NEW YORK, U.S.A.

S.S. SILVIA

In 1905 the S.S. *Silvia*, which provided a direct link between Newfoundland and New York, brought the five shipwrecked Conception Bay seamen home. Insignia for the Red Cross Line can be seen on her two stacks.

the vessel up somewhat. If *Gladys* sank beneath their feet, which they expected at any moment, they had no lifeboat to launch.

On the last day of the year 1904, the crew had no time to celebrate or ring out the old year. They worked with the desperation of doomed men, throwing cargo over the side and pumping. Water did not gain; thus one or two men could snatch a few hours sleep. No other ship had been sighted for over a day. To lighten *Gladys* further, the heavy port anchor and chain were dropped overboard. The next two days brought lighter winds, snow and high swells.

Then, at noon on Monday, January 3, when the beleaguered seamen least expected it, S.S. *Balakani* commanded by Captain Hewett, bore down on *Gladys*. Despite the white-

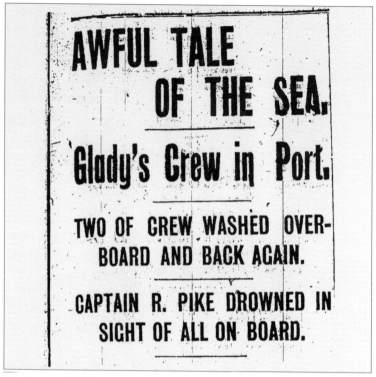

AWFUL TALE
OF THE SEA.

'Glady's Crew in Port.

TWO OF CREW WASHED OVER-
BOARD AND BACK AGAIN.

CAPTAIN R. PIKE DROWNED IN
SIGHT OF ALL ON BOARD.

This is how a *Daily News* story of January 1905 featured the arrival of *Gladys'* crew in St. John's.

capped swells, *Balakani* seamen launched the lifeboat, ploughed it over to the side of the wallowing schooner and took off the crew.

S.S. *Balakani* carried the Conception Bay mariners to Port Arthur, Texas, and from there they travelled to New York by train where they joined S.S. *Silvia* bound for St. John's.

They arrived in Conception Bay in mid-January 1905. According to the book *Sailing Vessels and Crews of Carbonear* (F. Saunders, 1981), when the news broke they were coming, flags flew half-mast on every ship and half-staff on every pole out of respect for Captain Reuben Pike and his family. The remaining five had saved only the clothes they stood in, but didn't complain, as they felt lucky to have escaped with their lives.

To verify the information in *Raging Winds...Roaring Sea* I used as many sources as possible: archival newspapers, diaries, gravestones, official crew or shipping lists, scrapbooks and tales told by people (or their descendants) who were directly involved.

With many early shipwrecks there is a shortage of reliable information. Few Newfoundland newspapers existed before 1900, and those that reported on marine tragedies often carried brief, impersonal details. Little was said of the families affected by the loss of a loved one; quite often the crew was not identified or their place of residence not given. This is true for the next story.

When I located and read, in American sources, of Captain Ben Pine's connection with the south coast I was intrigued. His biography is not included in the *Newfoundland Encyclopedia* or in editions of "Who's Who", but the New York *Times* carried an extensive obituary of Pine when he passed away. He was a Newfoundlander who made a name for himself in Massachusetts. From the great seaport of Gloucester, Captain Pine often sent his ships back to Newfoundland for cargoes. He was a mentor for young Newfoundland skippers. Ironically his successful enterprises and his rise to certain seafaring stature were overshadowed by two tragic shipwrecks.

This story was written in 1998 and submitted to the *Newfoundland Quarterly*'s feature "Prominent Figures from our Recent Past."

10 Disaster: One by Fire, One by Water

Marystown, Belleoram, Connaigre Peninsula

Twice this ship brought tragedy: by fire and by water. A schooner built, owned, and sailed from Gloucester, Massachusetts, twice claimed lives and each event had a south coast connection. The chain of events begins in 1912 when the one hundred thirty-seven ton fishing vessel christened *Mary* slipped down the ways at the Arthur D. Story shipyards at

Essex, Massachusetts. She fished out of Gloucester as the *Mary*, and later in her career, 1928, was re-christened *Arthur D. Story*.

How and why she changed her name in 1928 from *Mary* to *Arthur D. Story* is the crux of this tragic tale of the sea. It ends with the death of a Marystown sea captain John Farrell.

Captain Ben Pine was part owner of the *Mary*. Born in Belleoram, as a young man Pine learned the lore of the sea and emigrated to the United States. His brother Captain Frank Pine chose to remain in Newfoundland and in time commanded several local sailing ships — the *Adriatic, Vogue, Florence Swyers* and *Olive Moore*.

After Ben Pine emigrated to the United States, he worked his way up through the ranks and eventually commanded several Gloucester fishing schooners. Pine became a hero within the New England fleet, not only for his extraordinary catches of fish, but also because he commanded the fast and able *Columbia*, America's entry in International Fishermen's Races in which the famed Nova Scotian *Bluenose* went undefeated.

Our story at this point does not centre around Captain Pine, but a hard-working protegee of his, Captain John S. Farrell of Marystown (in one instance his middle initial was recorded as B). In the spring of 1928, Captain Farrell was to take *Mary* halibut fishing. Farrell, age thirty-seven, had also climbed the ladder of success within the realm of Gloucester skippers; in fact, a new vessel was to have been built for him that summer to replace the aging *Mary*.

Mary was due to sail the evening of May 30, 1928. Captain Farrell, while waiting for the remainder of his crew to arrive, went for a car ride with Pine through the streets of Gloucester. Farrell left instructions for *Mary*'s engineer to attend to the lighting system.

The devices providing electricity on early fishing schooners were crude. A small engine, similar to today's gas generators, produced enough electricity to light a dozen or so electric bulbs strung along the schooner's rigging and this, replacing the outmoded torch lanterns, enabled the crew to

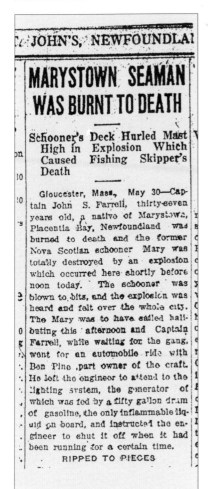

ST. JOHN'S, NEWFOUNDLAI

MARYSTOWN SEAMAN WAS BURNT TO DEATH

Schooner's Deck Hurled Mast High in Explosion Which Caused Fishing Skipper's Death

Gloucester, Mass., May 30—Captain John S. Farrell, thirty-seven years old, a native of Marystown, Placentia Bay, Newfoundland was burned to death and the former Nova Scotian schooner Mary was totally destroyed by an explosion which occurred here shortly before noon today. The schooner was blown to bits, and the explosion was heard and felt over the whole city. The Mary was to have sailed this afternoon and Captain Farrell, while waiting for the gang, went for an automobile ride with Ben Pino, part owner of the craft. He left the engineer to attend to the lighting system, the generator of which was fed by a fifty gallon drum of gasoline, the only inflammable liquid on board, and instructed the engineer to shut it off when it had been running for a certain time.

RIPPED TO PIECES

The June 5, 1928, *Daily News* reports the death of Captain Farrell

dress fish at night. Needless to say, early generators and small gas-driven engines caused problems aboard the wooden vessels. Many a schooner burned at sea as a result.

The small engine on *Mary*'s deck was fed by one of two fifty gallon drums of gasoline, the only flammable liquid on board. The drums were likely stored below deck or were lashed onto the after rail. Farrell instructed the engineer to shut the engine off after five or ten minutes. When he returned from his ride, Captain Farrell found the engineer on the wharf and the generator still running with thick fumes from the gas creeping over the ship. He went on board to attend to the matter himself. He went into the cabin (or hold) to pull the switch, but a spark fired the gas vapour, which exploded, ripping *Mary* to pieces. Parts of the deck were hurtled as high as the mast heads.

The thirty or so men — some of whom were *Mary*'s crew — standing on the wharf heard the skipper cry out, "Ben, for God's sake, help me!" Then pieces of deck debris came back down and crushed him. Flames from two drums of gas enveloped him and caught the schooner afire. Somehow the crowd extinguished the blaze and saved the vessel, but it was

Schooner *Mary* on her launch at Essex, Massachusetts, 1912.

too late for Captain John Farrell, the only person aboard. He was married with six children, the youngest but a week old.

Mary was nearly destroyed; the explosion was heard all over Gloucester, debris was thrown hundreds of feet along the waterfront and one piece went through a roof five hundred feet away. Captain Ben Pine narrowly escaped injury. As he was stepping onto the schooner, he stopped to chat with a friend and, a few seconds later, the explosion occurred.

The schooner *Mary* was deemed salvageable. Her decks and bulwarks were rebuilt and she lived to fish and to sail again. Perhaps to rid the schooner of any bad luck, Ben Pine re-christened her *Arthur D. Story*, after the original builder.

Arthur D. Story sailed for seven years. In the latter part of February 1935 *Story* anchored on the eastern side of the Connaigre Peninsula loading frozen herring. In those days herring, used for bait by the Gloucester fishing fleet, was frozen on wooden racks in many south coast Newfoundland towns. American schooners came in January and February to load up.

On Sunday March 3, 1935, *Arthur D. Story* left Belleoram

for Gloucester with a cargo of herring. An unexpected and vicious wind and snow storm probably claimed her life and all aboard. No one ever knew what happened to the ill-fated schooner, but there were those who said she may have collided with the Grand Bank schooner *Alsatian*. *Alsatian* left Harbour Breton the same day, sailed into the storm and disappeared with twenty-five crew, ten belonging to Harbour Breton and the remainder were from various towns in Fortune Bay.

When *Arthur D. Story* failed to show up in Gloucester when expected, it was first thought she was caught in ice fields near St. Pierre Bank and was working her way out of them. Gloucester papers of March 20, 1935, said she might be ice-locked for a month or more, until she worked free or the ice weakened. On March 27, a seaplane flew over the ice in search. A Norwegian steamer sighted a vessel resembling *Story*, locked in ice at a point estimated to be one hundred fifty miles east of Sable Island, between Banquereau and St. Pierre Bank. It was not *Arthur D. Story*; she disappeared without a trace — a mystery of the sea.

News of a Gloucester schooner lost with crew trickled into Newfoundland. It was known that Captain William L. Nickerson, age fifty and married with two children, had some south coast seamen with him, but no Newfoundland sources mentioned (or for that matter, knew) their names.

It was not until recently, when researchers in New England located crew lists, that the identification of her seven men became clear. With Captain Nickerson were Thomas J. Cove, cook William E. Wolfe, Philip McCue, Morris Fitzgerald, James Gould and engineer Ralph S. Fiander. Certainly the latter two or three names are common on the south coast. Gould, 26 years old, lived at 104 Duncan Street, Gloucester; Ralph Fiander, age 21, lived at 16 Oak Street, but most likely these young men were born in Belleoram. And to be sure someone, somewhere, knows about them.

According to local stories, while at Belleoram three of *Story*'s crew (probably Fitzgerald, Gould and Fiander) walked to St. Jacques and brought with them a tin of Ameri-

Captain Angus Walters (right) of the schooner *Bluenose* and Captain Ben Pine of *Columbia* and *Arthur D. Story*. The two were friendly competitors in the International Fishermen's Races.

can coffee, a rare commodity on the south coast in those days. While some recalled the coffee and the crew who brought it, others who saw the ill-fated vessel just before she left port believed she was loaded too deeply in the head with the frozen herring. This, they thought, would make her unstable in a storm.

It is not known how these marine calamities affected the career of Captain Pine, nor has the mysterious disappearance of *Arthur D. Story* been solved. At any rate, these two stories make a fascinating, but tragic twist of events surrounding the schooner *Mary* also known as the *Arthur D. Story*.

Although many ships have met their doom along the Labrador coast, not many sea stories have been written about marine disasters that happened along this stretch of rugged coastline of roughly 7900 kilometres. I too have had difficulty locating fresh and otherwise untold stories of the Labrador coast.

In my earlier books, there are accounts of south coast schooners (like the *Paloma* at Batteau, the *Charlie and Eric* near Hopedale, or the *Orion* lost with crew in the Strait of Belle Isle) which met with disaster while chasing the northern cod stocks. But otherwise, tales of wrecked steamers and coasting vessels on Labrador shores were more elusive. Perhaps because of a paucity of newspaper coverage, or on my long distance to travel, I didn't gather first person information of wreck and ruin. Also there was less schooner traffic on the coast than around Newfoundland's shores and fewer calamities. One excellent publication which deals with shipwrecks on the coast of Labrador is *The Angry Seas* by Captain Joseph Prim and Mike McCarthy — a book I heartily recommend to those interested in the marine history of our province.

Over the years, as I researched or wrote a Labrador sea story, I sent it to *Them Days* Magazine and several were published. Thanks to Doris Saunders, the indomitable editor and preserver of all things Labradorian, "*Bay Rupert*'s Salvage at the Clinker" made its first appearance in *Them Days*. With her permission it now appears in *Raging Winds...Roaring Sea*.

11 Bay Rupert's Salvage at the Clinker
Labrador, Cape Harrigan, Hopedale

"**W**recked Goods," the ad shouted, "salved from the *Bay Rupert* but now wrecked in prices." In November 1927 the Bon Marche clothing store in St. John's advertised clothes salvaged from the shipwrecked S.S. *Bay Rupert*. A thousand sweaters sold at over fifty percent off.

Courtesy of *Them Days* Magazine and Hubert Miles collection

Bay Rupert (above) grounded off Labrador on the Clinker Rocks, 1927.

The wrecked goods came from the Hudson's Bay Company ship *Bay Rupert* which on July 22, 1927, steamed north for Labrador. Laden with coal, shop supplies, dry goods — especially clothing — she headed for the Moravian Mission trading posts along the Labrador coasts.

Bay Rupert, a passenger and cargo steamer launched only sixteen months before, was especially designed to serve as a supply ship to northern Labrador ports. Her hull was strengthened for navigation through ice. Ice she could push through but not the ragged shoals and ledges of the ocean. On the night of July 22, while under full speed and at latitude 55.59 north, longitude 59.59 west, she struck the Clinker Rocks about fourteen miles north of Cape Harrigan.

Immediately the 3700 ton steamer began to pound heavily. At first her crew thought she would float free on the next high tide and to this end much deck cargo was thrown overboard. Chief engineer John Ledingham, a resident of St. John's, advised the captain that *Bay Rupert* was stranded amidships and was swaying or pivoting upon the rock. Perhaps she could be pulled off.

By Saturday July 23, although the sea was calm, she had partly filled with water. All passengers and several crew, as well as livestock — pigs and sheep — were carried to the Farmyards, islands situated about seven or eight miles from the ship. The crew rowed there, some using canoes which *Bay Rupert* carried, and set up tents on the island.

W.J. Carson, manager of Hudson's Bay Company, asked any available ships in the area to assist in transporting goods or to help free the stranded vessel. S.S *Moverin*, 360 miles southeast, proceeded to the site. Herbert J. Russell, general manager of the Newfoundland Railway, wired Captain Tavernor of S.S. *Kyle* requesting him to go to the site where *Bay Rupert* was stranded.

On August 2, a report came from the S.S. *Beothic* saying *Bay Rupert* had been pulled off the rock, a message quickly denied by Hudson's Bay Company. But the truth was none of the ships could free the stranded wreck. *Bay Rupert* was, by this date, officially pronounced a total wreck and abandoned. The *Reindeer*, an ocean-going salvage tug out of the Halifax Shipyards Limited, had been at the scene and could do nothing.

"*Bay Rupert*'s engines and boilers have lifted," said Captain Taylor of *Reindeer*. "They have been forced up by the boulder the steamer rests on and which had pierced her bottom. *Bay Rupert*'s seams have since opened up and she's in such a state there's but a slight chance of salvaging the cargo." On August 7, *Reindeer* left the sea off Labrador headed for St. John's.

Two ships from Newfoundland came to take the dry cargo off *Bay Rupert* and then she was officially abandoned. Local salvagers could take what they pleased. News quickly spread along the coast. Small boats left towns like Makkovik, Nain, and Hopedale, steamed to the site and tied on to the stem and stern of the derelict. By then *Bay Rupert* was down so low swells broke between the bridge and the forward section. Salvers had to wait for low tide to get down to the second deck to pull out wet and damaged goods.

One salvager at the site reported, "The ship was on the rock nine miles straight out from Cape Harrigan...We couldn't get down to the second deck. We got some furniture, cupboards and stuff like that, and some potatoes."

"By and by Dr. Grenfell came there in the *Strathcona* and

anchored alongside, on the same shoal. He came out to the *Bay Rupert* in a dory...They were getting coal from her and whatever else they could get out of the hold." The Rogers family of Fair Island, Bonavista Bay, who fished off the Labrador coast in those years, still treasures a spy glass salvaged from *Bay Rupert*.

John Dickers of Hopedale was there and recalled the salvage:

> We went down right in time when she was there...there was a lot of people here got stuff off her. We picked up a lot of stuff around Island Harbour, lard, flour, guns. Up around Aillik shore all them places...I don't know what the Hudson's Bay Company took off her. Dr. Grenfell had quite a bit of it on the *Strathcona II*. They had all kinds of guns and everything you could mention in that boat...
>
> They had them in wooden boxes. Them days they'd take them abroad and put them in a wooden box and roll them in oiled paper. They'd never hurt done up in hard grease.
>
> The crew came here and went out on the *Kyle*. They got off the ship on lifeboats about 20-22 mile from Hopedale. (Taken from *Them Days Magazine*, April 1999)

By early September in the freshening fall winds, the derelict slowly broke up, but her remains lay on the rocks for nearly a month. Along the coast near Hopedale goods, which had been under water and couldn't be reached by salvers, drifted on shore — clothes, flour and lard. "There was all kinds of stuff driving in. The little coves and harbours were full of it," someone claimed.

The wreck of *Bay Rupert* at the Clinker Rocks, while a great setback to the Hudson's Bay Company, proved a windfall to many residents along the Labrador coast. As for the Bon Marche store in St. John's, it advertised salvaged items: 200 men's cotton and wool sweaters, all sizes at $1.49 each; 100 boys' grey sweater coats, V-neck, button front at $1.10 each and 200 ladies sweaters (fancy designs) at $3.50 each.

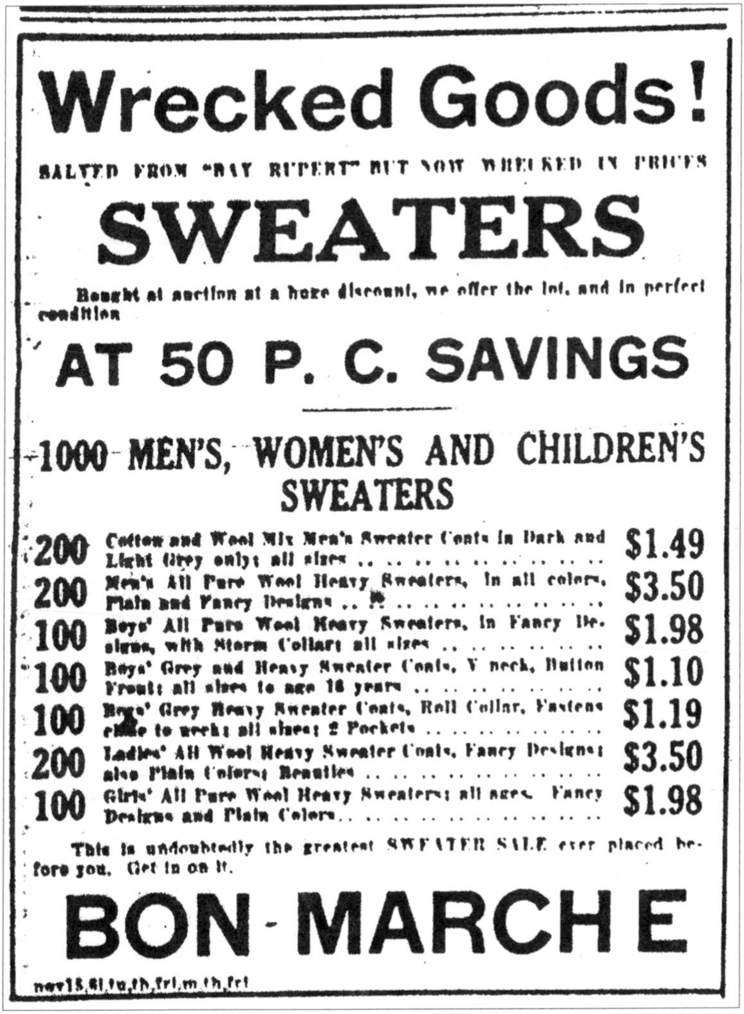

Wrecked goods from a wrecked ship, the *Bay Rupert*.

In February of 1999 Susanna (Douglas) Tucker, the daughter of Newfoundland sea captain Tommy Douglas, sent me information on a ocean voyage she took with her father in 1932. To my delight and surprise, she also sent two photos — one of Sue and her father and another of the schooner *Mark H. Gray*, the vessel they had sailed on together.

Sue Tucker's memories of sailing ships were unique and clear, as shown in this account. I knew this memoir was one to share with all and to this end I sent her story to the *Downhomer*. It was published in the March 2000 issue.

Several people, through e-mail, mail and phone calls, agreed that it was a singular and valuable description that helped preserve details of a by-gone way of life. Sue is perhaps one of the last surviving Newfoundland mariners to have voyaged to Europe on a sail-driven schooner. The Museum of the North Atlantic in Nova Scotia provided details on the construction and launching of *Mark H. Gray* in 1925. Their correspondence also shows that the correct spelling of the schooner is Gray, and not Grey as I had originally written in an earlier book.

12 A Girl's Trip to Europe by Sail

Fortune, Brunette, Gaultois

Sail-powered schooners last sailed out of Newfoundland ports over half a century ago and memories of them are but a fleeting vision in the minds of a few. The ranks of those who remember life on sailing ships, especially in the era when many South Coast ports were frequented by foreign-going schooners, are getting thinner with every passing day. Rare indeed are the recollections of a woman who when she was sixteen years old stood 'before the mast' on a sailing ship headed to Portugal.

In 1932, a trip overseas on a sailing vessel was the thrill of a lifetime for a young girl of Fortune, Newfoundland. Susanna "Sue" Douglas came from a seafaring family, and had seen the two-masters and tern schooners with their tall, sea-bleached sails leave home en route to exotic ports of call in faraway places: Cadiz, Oporto, Pernambuco, Maceio, Gibraltar and Magala.

Her father was Captain Thomas Douglas of Fortune who commanded foreign-going schooners on the trade routes from Newfoundland, the West Indies, Portugal and Spain. Often on the return voyage, his ship looked more weatherbeaten, especially in winter when Newfoundland crews had to battle severe mid-Atlantic storms.

Thomas Douglas, born on Brunette Island, Fortune Bay, rose through a seaman's apprenticeship until he eventually took charge of large schooners, like the tern *Ronald M. Douglas*, owned and operated by Garland's business in Gaultois. In time Captain Douglas married, lived and raised his family in Fortune. Sue's brothers — Fred, Clyde Lou, and Spencer — had gone on trips to Europe while teenagers. Perhaps Captain Douglas was initiating or preparing his family for a life at sea; at any rate they voyaged with him to Spain and Portugal for a summer vacation.

Sue Douglas sailed from Fortune in late June 1932 on the *Mark H. Gray*, a two-masted schooner jointly owned by Douglas and Garland's business. *Mark H. Gray*, laden with salt fish collected at Fortune and other Burin Peninsula ports, headed for Oporto, Portugal. It was a great excursion for father and daughter for, barring exceptionally stormy weather, they would be back home by late July or early August.

The journey, from Newfoundland to Europe and return, covered nearly 6000 miles; even with good weather the round trip would take four to six weeks. Summer crossings were relatively danger free, unlike the treacherous fall and winter trips when many Newfoundland schooners had disappeared in the stormy Atlantic, often ravaged by northwesterly gales. Sue's trip was two weeks eastbound and a little over three weeks return.

"We encountered a lot of stormy weather on the return voyage," she recalled.

Mark H. Gray sailed out through the ancient harbour of Fortune and as she glided past Fortune Head, the wind caught her mainsail, foresail, jib and jumbo. The schooner headed past Dantzic and Green Island, then left Fortune Bay behind. Sue could recall only two of *Gray's* five or six crew: her father and mate George Walters, who himself was a qualified sea captain.

The young sailor slept in the captain's after cabin which had two or three bunks, one of which was screened off for Sue's privacy. She ate in the galley or forecastle with the crew. The basic meals of pork and cabbage, salt cod, potatoes, fish and brewis were routinely served, but delicious. She also recalled the cook "making molasses biscuits or buns called lassie jimmies."

In stormy weather her father wisely tied a rope around her waist to prevent her from being washed overboard should an unexpected wave break across *Mark H. Gray's* deck. To be 'lashed to the wheel' or 'tied to life lines' while working on deck during ocean storms was common practise even for veteran sailors.

In two weeks her vessel arrived in Oporto, a city which South Coast sailors on foreign-going schooners had visited often since the 1900s. Oporto was the second largest city in Portugal, located up the Douro River. By the 1930s, its population was over a quarter million. The beauty and size of the busy city must have been a marvellous sight to a girl from a tiny Newfoundland fishing port.

"We were there about a week," Sue recalled. "Due to a problem on the wharf, we were not able to unload the fish and were re-routed to Lisbon." But Sue remembered staying in the ancient city of Oporto long enough to attend a bull fight with her father and a Captain Keeping from another South Coast schooner. Bull fighting, at that time as today, was a popular spectator sport attended by large crowds in one of several open air arenas.

They also went to an Oporto building called 'The Seaman's Rest' where Captain Douglas visited friends. A seaman's rest was a hostel or meeting place for British or

Courtesy Sue Tucker

Captain Thomas Douglas and his daughter taken by an Oporto photographer in 1932.

Newfoundland seamen. The structure, sometimes known as the Seaman's Home or Institute, was a hostel where seamen socialized, washed, cleaned up and lodged while in a foreign port. As proof of their stay in Oporto, Sue and her father visited a photographer, Nenes Guimares, to have their picture taken (see photo).

After a week's delay in Oporto while awaiting further instructions from shipping agents or brokers, Captain Douglas received orders to sail to Lisbon. For Sue, visiting two of the great seaports of Europe would be a topic of conversation with Fortune friends for years to come.

The young sailor fondly remembered, "We spent a week

Launched in 1925 from the Ernst yards at Mahone Bay, Nova Scotia, the schooner *Mark H. Gray* (above) netted 115 tons and was 134 feet long and 26 feet wide. Captain John Thornhill of Grand Bank, fishing for the LaHave Outfitting Company, was her first skipper. Her registry transferred to Newfoundland in May 1932.

in Lisbon. While there we went to see a very old castle that was built by the Moors. We also were taken on a tour of a vineyard owned by the salt fish brokers and given a case of port wine as a gift."

Lisbon and Oporto in 1932: what a cultural experience for a Newfoundland girl! Lisbon, situated on the Tagus River, was the capital and largest city of Portugal. The major industrial and commercial area of the country, it has an exceptionally fine harbour and in 1932 exported cork, canned fish, olive oil, resin and wine.

The city is built on the terraced sides of low hills. In the older section streets were narrow and crooked, but parts of Lisbon had, as today, straight, tree-lined avenues, attractive commercial squares and extensive public gardens. Sue must have marvelled at the Gothic cathedrals, old convents and monasteries, libraries and museums. The city had been held by the Moors of North Africa from the year 716 until it was retaken by the Portuguese in 1147. Indeed Sue visited remnants of a once-flourishing Moorish civilization.

When the cargo was discharged, *Mark H. Gray* took on a

load of salt and headed home. On the westward voyage adverse winds and occasional storms buffeted the schooner, but the weather was no worse than the captain and crew expected. When they reached the great fishing grounds, Grand Banks, the crew jigged fresh fish for supper. After such a voyage, when dried and salted food staples were getting low, a meal of fresh fish whether boiled, fried, or baked was a welcome treat. At last *Mark H. Gray* sailed along Newfoundland's south coast and into the friendly confines of Fortune harbour — everyone aboard safe and sound.

Alas, a reversal of fortunes, so common with families dependant upon the sea, turned pleasant memories into sad ones for Sue. A year later in the fall of 1933 *Mark H. Gray*, while on another voyage overseas, was posted "Missing at Sea, Lost with Crew." Apparently, the schooner with her five crew was overwhelmed by ocean storms while returning from Oporto laden with salt.

As Sue says, nearly seventy years after the event, "I remember the waiting and the watching as other ships returned. After several months we realized that our ship and the men were lost." Sue's grief was great. Her father, twenty-one year old brother Fred, and family friend George Walters were never seen again.

The stories — especially oral — of our past, our heritage and the events which shaped our rock-girt island are slipping away. With the one hundredth anniversary of the disappearance of *Mikado* it became my objective to publicize the events surrounding her loss in 1897. I wrote this story to perpetuate the memory of our island pioneers.

On April 2, 1997, I submitted *Mikado*'s story to the *Evening Telegram* by e-mail — my first submission for publication via that method of communication. It was printed on July 26, 1997, about the time when the excitement of the *Cabot 500* celebrations was at fever pitch. Thus, the story of the disappearance of Grand Bank's small ship may have been overshadowed by the appearance of John Cabot and his *Matthew*. Since first written, there is one other addition of vital importance — I located the remaining names of her crew in church records.

13 In the Waters of the Great Deep

Grand Bank

What is there today to remind us of the disappearance of the small ship *Mikado* and its crew in 1897? The physical evidence consists of a weathered gravestone in a Grand Bank cemetery, a newspaper clipping of sixty or seventy words, and a letter in an obscure church pamphlet.

Family tradition and oral retellings of community events are strong in outport Newfoundland, but today there is little retold of this schooner. None of the five crew survived, but the grandson of the captain is a prominent Newfoundlander and, for that reason alone, the story of the disappearance of *Mikado* deserves to be remembered. Perhaps, too, we should strive to preserve the events which helped develop our island home and helped shape towns like Grand Bank and its people.

In mid-October 1897, the thirty-seven ton *Mikado* left Grand Bank for Halifax, Nova Scotia, laden with dried cod.

She was owned and commanded by Thomas Alex Hickman, an experienced seafarer who had often skippered his own and other vessels. Named for the ancient rulers of Japan, or perhaps for the Gilbert and Sullivan operetta, *Mikado* had been built in Prince Edward Island in 1887. A two-masted schooner, she measured sixty feet long and eighteen feet wide. Quite possibly Hickman had seen and purchased the schooner on one of his previous fall trips to Prince Edward Island for produce. Being of shallow draft and designed to operate in coastal waters, such a small vessel may have been out of her element in the treacherous waters of the Gulf of St. Lawrence.

By the 1880s, many Grand Bank ship owners and merchants found it more profitable to deal with Canadian markets and did not ship fish to nor buy supplies from St. John's. Thus, when *Mikado* was laden with the fall-cured salt fish, she sailed for Halifax. After discharging cargo, the crew would head to Prince Edward Island to load produce (mainly potatoes, other vegetables and shop goods) for a new store Hickman had intended to open.

Thomas Alexander Hickman, who owned waterfront property on both sides of the harbour, had already decided to give up the sea and planned to establish a business in Grand Bank. Before the turn of the century, several of the town's mercantile firms were started by master mariners: Samuel Harris, J.B. Patten, Samuel Piercy and the Buffett business. But, fate intervened. When *Mikado* was ready to leave Grand Bank, her regular captain decided to stay ashore and Hickman had no alternative but to go in his place.

Mikado carried five crew, the usual complement for a coasting (trader) vessel of thirty-forty ton and all belonged to Grand Bank: Captain Hickman, age fifty-five, John Clarence Hickman, twenty-one, Robert Bond, nineteen, George Hickman and William Hynes.

Robert Bond was the youngest aboard. Robert's father, William, who lived in Grand Bank for many years after *Mikado*'s loss, spent the rest of his life grieving over his son's fate. It is said his heavy stock of black hair turned white within a few weeks after the schooner's disappearance when he knew his son had been claimed by the sea.

Exactly what happened will never be known. *Mikado* could have foundered in heavy seas, been pushed ashore on some remote rocky ledge, or may have capsized in a sudden gale. Well documented, though, is the sudden, violent windstorm that came up three days after she left home port. The storm, perhaps the tail-end of a tropical hurricane, overpowered the little schooner and her crew.

Captain Thomas A. Hickman, lost at sea 1897.

Those were the days of limited communication and after a vessel left home port often no news came back until she arrived home again. In vain, relatives waited. Perhaps another ship met *Mikado* and the captains exchanged reports, or maybe someone telegraphed Nova Scotia inquiring if the schooner had arrived. But the lack of news on Hickman and his crew was ominous.

On November 18, 1897, the *Daily News* voiced on paper what many believed. The newspaper reported the loss of *Mikado* with the lead "Another Schooner Missing" saying she had left Grand Bank three weeks previously and was long overdue. The brief article concluded that "it is possible she has been driven off course by the recent gales and it is to be hoped she will turn up safely." This was not to be.

Two months after the tragedy an item was printed in the *Methodist Monthly Greeting*, a magazine once published by the Newfoundland Conference of the Methodist (later United) Church. Issue Thirteen, 1897, reveals:

To: Editor of the Greeting

Dear Sir, - During that memorable gale of Sunday night, on the 18th October last, one of the most respected and honoured members of this community, Mr. Thomas Alex. Hickman, master of the schooner Mikado, en route to Halifax, found rest from his labours with all his crew, in the waters of the great deep. The departed one being known to many of your readers you will oblige by inserting the following letter of condolence sent to the widow by his brethren in Masonry, of Fidelity Lodge, of this place.

Yours truly,
W. P. Way
Grand Bank, December 27th, 1897

(The letter of condolence follows)

Hickman, a past master of the Masonic Lodge in Grand Bank, was one of the organization's founding members when freemasonry was brought to the town in 1876. The introductory and the condolence letter to the *Greeting* was signed by fellow lodge officers; many of whom were the leading local businessmen: Samuel Harris, Samuel Tibbo, George A. Buffett, George Grandy, Selby Parsons and Doctor Allan MacDonald, the master of the lodge.

The Hickman family were pioneers of the town. While there is no direct written evidence stating that they came to Grand Bank from St. Pierre in 1763 when the islands were ceded to France by England in the Treaty of Paris, there is strong family tradition to support it. In English census of the 1800s, the family is well established in Grand Bank. The local gravestone of Jonathan Hickman (Thomas' grandfather) shows he died in Grand Bank in 1848 at the advanced age of 100 years. Family accounts say Jonathan was in Grand Bank when famed English cartographer Captain James Cook surveyed the harbour and Newfoundland's South Coast in 1765.

Captain Thomas Alex Hickman's epitaph on a memorial stone in the Grand Bank Methodist cemetery reads simply: **Lost at sea Oct 17, 1897, Age 55,** but the pangs of sorrow were deep. For extended family support in this time of shock and sadness, his wife, Maria (Forsey) had several sisters, one of whom became the grandmother of the late Senator Eugene Forsey. Maria had seven children to support, five girls and two boys: Jacob, who himself disappeared at sea in 1911 on the *Dorothy Louise*, and Percival.

Percival Hickman (1886-1966), age eleven when his father disappeared, served overseas in World War I with the Edmonton highlanders, a kilted regiment. In 1919 he returned home to found and manage the Western Marine Insurance Company, a successful Grand

His body claimed by the waters of the great deep; his stone lies in the Fortune Road Methodist Cemetery, Grand Bank

Bank based business which went into voluntary liquidation in the late 1950s with the decline of sailing vessels.

An amateur historian and diarist, Percival often talked to others and recorded past events in the emerging town. In 1979, a concise article on the history of Grand Bank written by Percival Hickman was published in *The Newfoundland Quarterly*.

One of Percival Hickman's two sons was named for his paternal grandfather, lost at sea twenty-eight years previously. Thomas Alexander Hickman attended and graduated from the U.C. Academy in Grand Bank, studied law and was admitted to the Newfoundland Bar in 1948. He served as a Member of the House of Assembly for Burin district from 1966 to 1975, for the Grand Bank district from 1975 to 1979 and was Minister of Justice and Attorney General for about ten years. In 1979, following his career in political life, the Honourable T. Alex Hickman became Newfoundland's Chief Justice.

The disappearance of *Mikado* became one sea tragedy of many to visit a town that derived its sustenance from the bounty of the ocean. Now shrouded in the mists of time, the unfinished log of Captain Thomas Alex Hickman's final voyage began a little over one hundred years ago, October 1897.

Occasionally, during the search for new or fresh material, one comes across an unusual incident of which there is little documentation in local newspapers. The outline or "bare bones" for story fourteen comes from family knowledge and anecdotal information. No Newfoundland newspaper interviewed several Burgeo seamen when they arrived home from Europe after Armistice Day, 1918. They had been captured from their foreign-going tern *Duchess of Cornwall* and imprisoned for two years in a German concentration camp. For several months kinfolk in Burgeo assumed they had been lost at sea.

No doubt at the time they were deservedly regarded as heroes in Newfoundland, but only one factual or "official" account appears in newspapers of the day. This is with the only non-Newfoundlander of *Duchess'* crew. Equally important are the memoirs related by a survivor when he was well up in years.

Three basic sources were used for this tale of our undaunted pioneers — newspaper *Western Star* "Legion Corner" August 13 and 20, 1960, the *Evening Telegram* of March 20, 1917, and Arthur Barter's memoirs as related by his grandson, Clayton Hutchings of British Columbia.

14 Men of Burgeo Rendezvous with the Enemy
Burgeo, English Harbour West, St. John's

In 1901 the tern schooner *Duchess of Cornwall* slipped down the ways at Burgeo, one of the first terns, or three masted schooners, built on Newfoundland's south coast. Owned by the Burgeo and Lapoile Export Company, the *Duchess* (as she was called locally), netted 129 tons and measured 105 feet long.

While no photo of her launch or stay in Burgeo could be located, there exists a picture of her last few minutes afloat. The photo was taken by the enemy at the time — German seamen who had just planted bombs under her keel. How the photo and the story of her survivors were passed down through the years is perhaps as intriguing as the sinking of *Duchess of Cornwall* itself.

Her loss was briefly mentioned in *Lost at Sea* (1991), but since that time other information has come to light and a more fleshed out story needs to be told, a story often related by crewman Arthur Barter and passed on through his grandson, Clayton Hutchings.

Built to carry fish to Europe and Brazil, the *Duchess* plied the Atlantic for many years with only one noteworthy incidents. In 1914, while on a voyage from Bahia, Brazil, to Newfoundland, Captain John Collier of Burgeo, who had a chronic kidney complaint, died on board. His two sons sailed with him and they had the heart-rending experience of burying their father at sea. Mate Leonard Hare finished *Duchess'* voyage back to Burgeo.

In early December 1916 *Duchess of Cornwall* made her last journey; she was then under the management of Burgeo's J.T. Moulton's business and commanded by Thomas Gunnery. She loaded salt fish at St. John's and headed to Europe. The company knew they took a risk, since the Atlantic was patrolled by unfriendly German U-boats or armed raiders. But Moultons had a backlog of fish to deliver and other ships had slipped over and back without getting caught.

In 1916, the enemy war effort at sea was increasing. Submarine warfare and naval blockades using armed raiders were part of a strategy to help Germany win a war. A naval blockade would bring a starved Europe to its knees. On December 8, four days after she left Newfoundland, a German merchant cruiser intercepted *Duchess*.

This cruiser-raider was in all likelihood the *Moewe*. To describe *Moewe*'s actions it is necessary to interject into the story of *Duchess of Cornwall* the fate of a St. John's vessel, Crosbie and Company's tern schooner *Jean*. On March 26, 1917, Crosbies received a message from their London agents that *Jean* had been sunk by the German raider *Moewe* and that her crew was held as prisoners of war in Germany.

Five months previous to this distressing telegram, *Jean* had left St. John's for Pernambuco (now Recife), Brazil, with a cargo of fish in drums. After delivering it, she sailed east with a cargo of tobacco destined for Lisbon. At Lisbon she was to load salt for Newfoundland, but as ill-luck would have it, *Jean* was spotted by *Moewe*. By then *Jean* had been one hundred days unreported. Relatives in St. John's and Carbonear, thinking she had been swallowed up a mid-Atlantic storm, feared for the safety of her crew: Captain Edgar Burke, mate John Doody, bosun Ted Merrigan, seamen Thomas Colford and Peter Cullen, all of Carbonear. Seaman Samuel Newell and cook William Kenny were from St. John's. There was also a stowaway aboard, Matthew Prim age thirteen, whose parents lived in St. John's. *Jean*'s crew was released when the war ended.*

Subsequent reports claimed *Moewe* had captured twenty-two steamers and five sailing ships (two of which were *Jean* and probably *Duchess of Cornwall*). The total tonnage sunk by the German raider was one hundred twenty-three thousand gross tons of shipping.

Duchess of Cornwall carried six men on her last trip: twenty-eight year old Captain Gunnery, cook Alfred Anderson, seamen Arthur Barter, George Crant, and Isaac Anderson, all from Burgeo and area. The navigator and mate was Peter Otterson, a native of Norway. He was a captain in his own right, but sailed on *Duchess* as a navigator, as all Newfoundland sailing ships were required to carry a certified navigator on overseas voyages.

It was Otterson who reached St. John's on March 20, 1917, and related the amazing story of what happened to *Duchess of Cornwall*, how and where her crew was imprisoned, and why he alone had returned to Newfoundland. According to Otterson, *Duchess* left St. John's with four thousand quintals of Labrador cod and was to proceed to Gibraltar for further orders. About eight hundred miles south of Cape Race on December 8, 1916, at seven o'clock in the morning, the crew spied a strange ship.

At first it was thought to be a westward bound tramp

---

* Captain Joseph Prim of St. John's is the son of Matthew.

steamer. *Duchess of Cornwall* was making good speed in a favourable wind, but the steamer bore down near the Burgeo tern and an officer ordered Captain Gunnery to stop. Gunnery and his men soon realized it was a German raider. Otterson described what happened next:

> An officer of this craft, with sixteen men fully armed, came on board and demanded our ship's papers, which were handed him by Captain Thomas Gunnery. The nature of her cargo and her British register were all the Huns required.
>
> [We] were given fifteen minutes to clear out of our ship and get on board the raider. A bomb was placed in the cabin and two others over the side of the ship. The officer lit the fuse and in less than a few minutes there was a loud explosion and twenty minutes after *Duchess of Cornwall* went under with all her light canvas set.

Otterson, in his story to the *Evening Telegram*, did not know the name of the raider, but stated that he and his crewmates were ordered to keep below deck. There were other prisoners already on the raider: the crews of three steamers which had met a similar fate to *Duchess of Cornwall*. For five days the men were confined to a small compartment under terrible conditions. Otterson continued:

> [We] were then transferred to the S.S. *Yarrowdale*, which was seized while en route from New York to Havre with general cargo. On board were five hundred sailors comprising the crews of a number of ships sent to the bottom by the pirate. No one was allowed the slightest freedom, being under an armed guard and forced to stay below deck.
>
> There was only one cook on board *Yarrowdale* to prepare for 500. Eighteen days after boarding, the latter ship reached Swinemunde where all prisoners were confined to barracks for five days. From there we were placed on trains and taken to Neusterlitz in the centre of Germany and again put in barracks which had recently been erected with accommodations for 5000.

Peter Otterson concluded his harrowing tale of capture, imprisonment and deprivation saying, "The victims suffered untold hunger and were allowed practically nothing but bad bread and water. We were not asked to work." Before long however, Otterson claimed his liberty as a citizen from the neutral country of Norway. On January 27, 1917, along with twenty-three of his countrymen and three Americans, he was sent to Copenhagen, Denmark.

From there he wired the shipowners in Newfoundland informing them of the loss of *Duchess of Cornwall* and the capture of her crew. Otterson proceeded to Bergen, Norway, where he stayed for two weeks, and then obtained permission from the British Consul to join a British freighter. Otterson crossed over to Hull, England. He was given a passage to Liverpool, joined an Allan liner for Saint John, New Brunswick, and finally reached St. John's via a ship sailing from Louisbourg, Nova Scotia. Four months had elapsed since he left St. John's on the *Duchess*. Since Otterson, upon release from prison, chose to leave Norway and return to Newfoundland, it is likely he resided or was employed in St. John's.

Otterson thought that basic food supplies in Germany were so bad and in such short supply that the German people were on the verge of a huge uprising. He believed that at any moment a revolution more violent than the recent Russian revolution would occur.

It is here "official" or newspaper reports of the fate of *Duchess'* crew ends and Arthur Barter's personal tale, albeit brief, begins. Arthur Edward Barter was born in Cape La-Hune and began his sea life as a young man sailing on Burgeo schooners. When he sailed on *Duchess of Cornwall's* last journey he was twenty years old. In later years he often told others — especially his grandson Clayton Hutchings — the story of his ship's loss and his subsequent imprisonment in Germany.

When the enemy ship stopped the *Duchess*, Barter and his crew mates were given a few minutes to abandon their schooner. In that time they had to grab what was necessary to

Burgeo tern schooner *Duchess of Cornwall* in her last moments. Bombs have been planted and a lifeboat makes its way back to the German cruiser.

survive on the ocean, launch the dory and get off. Fortunately the sea at the time was relatively calm.

Barter's personal recollections differ slightly from the newspaper for the paper reports a boat load of German sailors rowed over and planted bombs. Barter recalls that *Duchess of Cornwall* was shelled. At any rate the Burgeo schooner was soon on the bottom and German ship left the scene of destruction. The six crew — five Newfoundlanders and one Norwegian — were alone in the mid-Atlantic in a small dory.

But, in a gesture of humanity, the German captain returned to inform the Newfoundland seamen that he had heard on his wireless a bad storm was in the forecast. He said to Captain Gunnery, Barter and the others that they probably would not survive the storm. Land was hundreds of miles away. If they wished they could come aboard his already crowded ship, but would be taken to Germany as prisoners of war.

The helpless crew decided it was better to be alive and in prison than to die by drowning or exposure within a few days. Relatives and friends would never know what had happened to them.

As it turned out, they stayed on this ship for awhile until transferred to a larger vessel — the British steamer *Yarrowdale*, captured by the Germans as a "war prize." Manned by German sailors and filled with crews of other sunken ships, she headed to Germany. Barter recalled that he and his crew mates ended up in a prisoner of war camp outside Brandenberg — one hundred twenty kilometres from Neusterlitz, where Otterson was located.

They all survived (although Barter makes no mention of crews of other ships brought to Germany on *Yarrowdale* or of other prisoners) and were released when the war ended. While Barter and his Burgeo friends were in the camp, the German sea captain — probably the man who commanded *Yarrowdale* — visited them several times bringing them food and cigarettes. When the war ended on November 11, 1918, the German skipper invited Barter and others into town where they celebrated with a good meal, a few beers and laughter. The whole group posed for pictures. It was early 1919 when the Burgeo men arrived home.

For years after, Barter and the captain exchanged Christmas cards, until about 1974 when he received a letter from the German skipper's daughter informing him her father had died. In the latter part of his life Barter lived in Corner Brook with his family and he joined the Corner Brook Royal Canadian Legion. Captain Gunnery moved to Halifax. The other crew lived in Burgeo and, undaunted by their experiences, continued to follow the sea. It is not known what happened to Captain Peter Otterson.

The Burgeo men had an unusual experience, but they were not the only south coast crew captured on the high seas and imprisoned in Germany. *Dictator*, a schooner owned on Newfoundland's south coast, fell prey to a German submarine in July 1918. Treatment of Captain Tom Fiander, of English Harbour West, and his five crew in a POW camp was not so pleasant. Before the incarceration ended two died, Leo Bungay of pneumonia, and James Parsons was killed by a train near the camp.

For the details on this story I am grateful to Leonard Long's grandson, Floyd Priddle of Milltown, Baie d'Espoir, who sent me the basic story. Harold Simms of Norwell, Massachusetts, whose grandfather helped build *Wilfred L. Snow*, provided statistics on the schooner's size and date of construction. I searched the archival newspapers for the loss of the schooner but nothing could be found.

I would have been delighted to have located more information in newspapers on the loss of the *Snow*. I realize pertinent printed information that I attempted to find on this and others stories in *Raging Winds...Roaring Sea* may exist. Some future researcher may find and expand on the gaps I have not been able to adequately fill. But part of the satisfaction that comes from presenting sea tales like this is the search for answers; then there is gratification for spending countless hours in archives and museums. When the pieces fit together, the musty past becomes a little clearer.

15 *Thanks Be to God and a Barking Dog*
St. Albans, Burgeo

When the three crew of *Wilfred L. Snow* finally reached shore after seventy-two hours in a dory, they were delirious and near death. Their lives were saved through their endurance and will to live and also through circumstance or sheer luck.

But their story, like most Newfoundland epics of the sea, begins with a ship — the ubiquitous schooner that was used everywhere around our rock-bound coasts a little more than a generation ago.

Wilfred L. Snow's beginnings were unusual. When she slipped down Joseph McGill's ways at Shelburne, Nova Scotia in 1905, she was the first schooner with an engine launched from the yards. Designed by the famous yacht designer Crowinshield of Boston and built for Captain Edward Keans of Lower Granville, Nova Scotia, *Wilfred L. Snow* was chartered to fish out of Digby in the Bay of Fundy.

Wilfred L., as she came to be called, measured seventy foot in overall length with a seventeen foot beam and netted thirty-five ton. Equipped with a twenty horsepower kerosene engine, she required no topmasts. In heavy wind her sails powered the ship, but in light wind and calm the crew relied on the engine, thus she was termed an auxiliary/sail schooner, the first auxiliary fishing schooner in Digby.

In time, *Wilfred L. Snow*'s registry transferred to Newfoundland, first to Allan Collins of Newtown, Bonavista Bay, who acquired her in 1925. Then in 1931 John Penny and Sons of Ramea purchased the vessel.

When her final sea misadventure occurred she was owned by Leonard Long who had bought *Wilfred L. Snow* in 1941 from Penny for eighteen hundred dollars — a new schooner built in Newfoundland would have cost Long about eight thousand dollars. By that time the kerosene burning engine had been replaced with two twenty-horsepower engines, although one was an Atlantic engine, the other Acadian.

Captain Leonard Long, like most businessmen who owned a small schooner, took cargo and freight of any description for this was the way of the sea and, as well, it kept a few dollars coming in.

Based out of St. Alban's, Bay d'Espoir, Captain Long bought scrap metal from folks along the coast: old stoves, steel drums, tin and copper. Long sold his metal at North Sydney and, as was his usual custom, purchased coal at North Sydney for the return voyage.

His last run in 1952 — and as it turned out the final voyage for the old workhorse schooner — began from Sydney on October 5 under blue skies and fair winds. Long, age forty-six, had with him two hard working seamen from the south coast, Joseph Davis, age twenty-one, also of St. Albans and Aloysius Benoit of Conne River, also around twenty-one.

About forty-five miles west southwest of Channel Head, Port aux Basques, *Wilfred L. Snow* began to leak around the rudder case. Presumably the stuffing box (or packing box) had loosened. A stiff wind had blown up since early morning.

When Long discovered the leak, he set up a rotary pump which drew power from the engine, but seawater poured in faster than the pump could keep it out. Soon water swamped the engine, rendering the electric pump useless.

"Man the hand pumps!" It was five o'clock in the evening; both engines were out and the wind had strengthened to forty miles an hour. Seas were high and rough, rain was light, but occasionally the evening sky was lit by lightning.

"I don't feel much like getting out into a dory into those seas," each man must have thought as they tried to save the old schooner. The *Wilfred L.* was now settling by the port bow. As she listed more and more the deck load of coal shifted and slid over the port side taking the railing and two drums of fuel with it. Long had aboard a wood stove purchased in Nova Scotia for his brother Lawrence; that too went to the bottom.

Only the dory, which had been lashed down, remained on deck, but was damaged. Aloysius Benoit made some quick repairs. Loss of the deck cargo lightened the schooner somewhat but soon *Wilfred L. Snow* listed worse than before. There was no ship-to-shore aboard, only a small radio, but the vessel was out of range of any broadcast.

With the hatches battened down, it was difficult to get to the coal in the holds in order to jettison the heavy cargo over the side. By seven o'clock waves washed over the deck. Soon it seemed obvious; it was time to abandon ship. Trouble stared them in the face: high winds and waves, a small dory and darkness. And how far away was nearest land?

Eight P.M. October 5, 1952, etched itself painfully into long term memory. In the darkness and through the storm, Long, Davis and Benoit did not see the forty-five year old sea soldier make its final dip. All charts, maps, logs and papers disappeared with the ship, but Captain Long salvaged the compass although, without a light, it was of little use the first night.

They realized they had a long pull to land and the strong north northwest wind was against them. With each white-cap, plenty of water poured into the dory. Bailing was a constant chore. By two A.M. the storm eased somewhat, but the air was cold.

They soon fashioned a drogue or "drug" with some two by four planks they had brought from the sinking schooner. These were tied together, thrown over the stern and soon the drag made it easier to keep the dory's nose into the wind. Other than the three castaways, there was little in the dory: two sets of oars, thwarts, a bit of lumber, and some canned water which they soon found out was unfit to drink.

The last food each hungry man had consumed was about dinner time Thursday; now it was breaking daylight Friday. Battling cold, bailing water, and rowing constantly exhausted each man. But their ordeal was far from over.

The weather turned more severe by mid-day and each man complained of blisters on the hands and buttocks. After a cold, wet and sleepless night, there were no dry clothes to change into. And row they must or be capsized and never see land.

As dusk fell Friday evening exhaustion, dehydration, and starvation set in. Often when a human wearies past the point of endurance, hallucinations mix with reality. Captain Leonard Long swore he saw elephants floating in the cloudy sky; each man saw ghostly ships in the air and on the water, each one travelling in a different direction. The ships seemed so real, they tried to summon several, but soon gave up in exhaustion.

On October 7, their bodies refused to function: cramps, sores, aches, blisters on fingers, hands, arms, legs, feet and buttocks broke. Tongues and throat were so dry, it was difficult to speak. Yet they persisted, rowed on and hoped for salvation. On late Saturday afternoon Aloysius Benoit dropped his oars and ducked down, shouting, "Get down, Get down. That's a low bridge we're passing under." But it was no bridge, only an illusion shimmering the salty air.

At dawn the next day, all three were lying on the bottom of the dory, waiting. For what? Salvation? Yes! Death? Maybe! Winds and fate were with them. The wind was onshore and by nightfall the little craft ground on a sandy

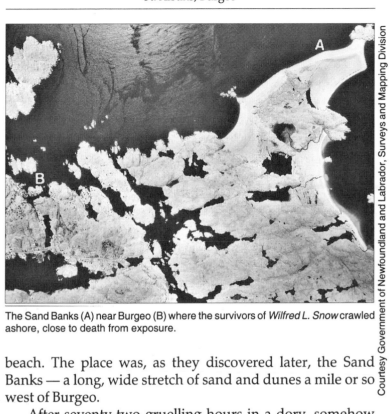

The Sand Banks (A) near Burgeo (B) where the survivors of *Wilfred L. Snow* crawled ashore, close to death from exposure.

beach. The place was, as they discovered later, the Sand Banks — a long, wide stretch of sand and dunes a mile or so west of Burgeo.

After seventy-two gruelling hours in a dory, somehow they found the strength to clamber out and to pull it up a little distance on the beach. Each helped the other get out of their oilskins before collapsing on the beach. Just up the beach Captain Long saw a clothesline filled with drying clothes, but when he finally crawled near, it was another cursed illusion in the form of a large white rock.

It is unlikely they would have survived the night, but fate can be cruel or kind and this time the hand of providence turned favourably toward them. George Barter, a sixty year old Burgeo man, had been hunting around Connoire and was now heading back home in his dory with a "make and break" engine. It was almost dark and, to help him navigate the sea safely, he hugged the shoreline. As he passed the Sand Banks, the little dog he had with him stood in the front of the dory and began to bark furiously.

"What is it, Blackie? Do you see something?" said Barter to his dog. "Lie down and be quiet!" But the dog barked louder and to George Barter it seemed to have caught the scent of something. The man had not bagged many birds that evening, so perhaps the dog smelled birds or rabbits near the shore. George Barter pulled upon the beach to check it out.

In the gathering darkness he found a weather beaten dory. Curious, he looked farther up the beach and almost stumbled over three bodies lying face down in the wet sand. "I think they're alive," he thought and bent down. Soon the three began mumbling. From the incoherent speech, Barter learned bits and pieces of their story.

But there was no time to waste. "Quick, pass me your oilskins, sir," he said. "I'll store them in the head of my dory." Benoit was so disoriented, he picked up the small black dog and passed it over to Barter.

Barter kindly helped them into his dory, tied on *Wilfred L. Snow*'s dory to the stern, and hastily headed for Burgeo, a mile or two away. An hour later, local men lifted Leonard Long, Joe Davis and Aloysius Benoit onto to the wharf while others went to get help from the local detachment of the RCMP. The police carried them to the Burgeo hospital.

For the first two days, each castaway was given about a teaspoon of water and the same amount of food every hour. This amount was slowly increased until October 11 when they ate their first solid meal. A warm bath was certainly welcomed as were clean, dry clothes and a soft bed to sleep in. And sleep they did.

On October 13, they were released and reached home on the S.S. *Baccalieu*. The dory — the last remaining artifact of the schooner *Wilfred L. Snow* — was kept at Burgeo by the RCMP and the next spring Wilson Riggs of McCallum brought it to St. Albans.

Thus three hardy sailors of Newfoundland's south coast, through the sheer dint of perseverance, survived. But fate or luck had a hand too when a favourable wind, a disappointed hunter and a barking dog combined to save lives.

In August 1999, I received a letter from Bruce Warr of Robert's Arm, a local historian and keeper of family traditions. Bruce told me the basic story of the loss of *Swallow* and later sent information on the Warr shipbuilders and others details of *Swallow*. Armed with the knowledge and date of her wreck, I searched archival papers, including *New York Times* and Newfoundland's *Evening Telegram*. Information was adequate enough to piece together a brief history of the ill-fated Newfoundland schooner.

This story appeared in the *Evening Telegram* on the January 18, 2000, on the anniversary of *Swallow*'s loss.

16 Pilley's Island Launch; Long Island Demise
Pilley's Island, Robert's Arm

*T*his tale of ships and shipbuilding begins on Pilley's Island, but the final episode ends on the front pages of the *New York Times*. The *Times* headlines of January 18, 1909, read **Ship's Crew of 12 Lost in Storm off Sandy Hook, New York**. It's a tragic story of the sea that has its roots on Pilley's Island, Notre Dame Bay.

Born in Twillingate, George Warr was a shipwright in the town of Pilley's Island, Notre Dame Bay. Family tradition says he built a total of forty-two vessels, ranging in size from small boats and schooners to foreign-going tern schooners. Indeed the Warr family made a name for itself as skilled shipwrights and carpenters. Another noted builder in the Warr lineage was Frank Warr. George was a nephew of Frank and it was from Frank he learned the shipbuilding trade. Frank moved from Twillingate to Robert's Arm before the turn of the century and there he built several vessels including one called *Salvationist*, used as a mission boat by the Salvation Army for many years. He also built the fifty foot long *Lullworth*, launched in 1884 at Robert's Arm.

But it's a ship built by George Warr that is the focal point for this Newfoundland tale of the sea. Names and details of

Seven crew pose on the side of *Swallow* (above). Land in the background is Pilley's Island, near the wharf of Michael Whalen's business. *Swallow* was built in a cove near Guy's Point, on the western entrance to Pilley's Island.

the many vessels built by George are scanty except one: the two-masted, eighty-five ton *Swallow*, launched in spring of 1908 and owned by C.F. Taylor. Several of Warr's vessels were named for birds, i.e. swallow, bluebird, eagle.

After a successful summer fishing on the Labrador, in the fall *Swallow* was chartered to carry a cargo of herring to the United States. Laden with casks in her hold and lumber on deck, she left Green Bay, Newfoundland, on her first voyage to foreign waters.

Captain George C. Daggett, an American agent who supervised the barrelling of the herring in Green Bay, chartered *Swallow* to take his cargo to Gloucester. Off northeastern Newfoundland *Swallow* encountered stormy weather and stopped at St. John's for minor repairs. There Daggett left to travel by train to Port aux Basques and thence to America to find a market for the herring before the schooner arrived.

Jeweller Joseph Roper's advertisement, circa 1909, for watch repairs. He also was Newfoundland's leading repairman for ship chronometers. The Roper family hailed originally from Bonavista. William Henry Roper, Joseph's brother, was lost on the S.S. *George Cromwell* when she disappeared off Cape St. Mary's, January 1877. John Roper was a magistrate in Bonavista.

Before leaving Daggett inquired around St. John's for a replacement captain for *Swallow* and subsequently hired Francis "Frank" Morris, age twenty-eight, of Robinson's Head (today called Robinsons), St. George's Bay. On the morning of departure Captain Morris took the ship's compass to Roper's Compass and Watch establishment to have it examined or replaced. Joseph Roper, considered at the time to be the best clock repairman, compass and chronometer specialist in Newfoundland, found no problem with the compass, but suggested the fault was in the schooner's binnacle, or receptacle for the compass. It probably had more iron on one side than the other and this, according to Roper, threw the compass off by several degrees. Being in a hurry to

sail, the captain could not wait to have the necessary altera-
tions made. *Swallow* left St. John's that evening.

Other crew aboard *Swallow* were cook William Rice of
Pilley's Island; Elihu Patey, St. Anthony; mate Charles Har-
mish, age twenty-five, of Liverpool, Nova Scotia and two
other unidentified seamen probably from the United States.
Apparently *Swallow* reached Gloucester in mid-January,
1909, and was ordered to sail to New York to discharge cargo.

The next news of the Newfoundland vessel came early
Monday morning, January 18, 1909 when New York newspapers reported an unknown ship (later identified as the schooner *Swallow*) stranded on the sand bar off Long Island, fifteen
miles east of Fire Island.

On the previous evening, Sunday, a coastal patrolman
from the Blue Point station saw a hull of a ship aground.
Breakers rolled over the vessel, at times obscuring her from
sight. As far as could be seen in the gathering darkness, the
craft was on her beam ends and pounding heavily. On
Sunday morning, when the ship struck, there had been a
blinding snowstorm.

On Monday morning, as the group of lifesaving men
gathered on the shore near the wreck, debris drifted ashore
which identified the derelict as *Swallow*, port of registry St.
John's. Darkness and high seas prevented the shore patrol
from launching a lifeboat. Every wave brought in pieces of
her timbers and planks, barrels of frozen herring and other
debris. Late in the evening her mast drifted in as well as an
undamaged dory. The reefer coat and other articles of clothing found a quarter mile from the scene led authorities to
believe no one had survived. Thirty rescue men, thwarted by
high seas from doing the job they were trained for, patrolled
the shore in the snow and rain waiting for bodies to wash
ashore. None were recovered.

From what could be determined of her final hours, *Swallow* was caught in a storm as she tried to shelter near Sandy
Hook. It was possible the crew, visibility obscured by drifting
snow, lost their bearings and grounded. Others speculated
that frozen spray coated the rigging making it impossible to

work the ship free from the land. *Swallow* was insured for $4,500; its cargo at $5000.

Headlines from January 18, 1909 *New York Times* correctly reported the loss of a Newfoundland schooner, but erroneously gave the number of crew as twelve. Her crew had three Newfoundland men, one from Nova Scotia and two whose names or place of residence were not recorded.

I like to get out to local craft fairs and book stalls to promote (and of course sell) my books. But something else happens at book promotions in places like St. John's, Bonavista, Marystown, Grand Bank and Grand Falls. There I meet the people who know the stories and are the descendants of our seafaring ancestors. Often they will ask me if I have heard or have written of a particular seaman, ship, wreck, town or story. From that contact with Newfoundland's great storytellers come unique and valuable tales of our hardy pioneers, information that would otherwise be lost.

Such is the case of Margaret (Strickland) Grant whom I met in Mount Pearl. She told me of her father, William Strickland, and his indomitable will to survive. In addition there was written documentation of his ordeal on the sea. It is to thoughtful people like Margaret, that I dedicate this next story — one which both Margaret and I cherish. "Adrift" is longer than most selections in *Raging Winds...Roaring Sea.* I have broken it into sections for ease of reading. But William's Strickland's memoir of survival is well worth the length.

17 Adrift: William Strickland's Story
Spaniard's Bay, Burin, Ramea, South Coast

*W*illiam Thomas Strickland's escape from death on the ocean was so traumatic and memorable he felt compelled to write and publish his story in a book for all to read. *Adrift*, a slim volume of twenty pages, was published in St. John's in 1900 with the encouragement of friends and the support of businesses.

Stories of men adrift in dories from Newfoundland schooners are many. These men, usually two to a boat, rowed away from the mother ship to fish. Many disappeared forever. Others, more lucky, rowed or drifted for days until they reached shore or another vessel. They existed on little food and water, exposed to the Atlantic's worst elements and suffered from cold, sleep deprivation, exposure, hunger and thirst.

Scores of Newfoundland dory fishermen (estimated to be in the hundreds although the exact number may never be known) perished; possibly their small craft overturned or was swamped with waves, or the men passed away before the drifting dory was found. Others survived; they had the indomitable strength of body and mind to stick it out for a few more hours, another day. Sometimes one lived while the other died, usually of exposure or thirst.

Such is the tale of William Strickland of Spaniard's Bay as told in *Adrift*, written three years after his death-defying experiences on the North Atlantic. "It is at the request of many friends," he begins, "that I am writing the story of my sufferings and escape from death."

April 1897, Schooner Lily of Burin William Strickland, twenty-one years old and single, left Spaniard's Bay in April 1897 and went to St. John's to look for work. On April 25th he and his friend, William Butt of Spaniard's Bay, sailed on one of Goodfellow's boats for Burin where both men had secured employment as dory fishermen on the schooner *Lily*.

Lily, a thirty-one ton vessel owned and captained by William Goddard, was built in Burin in 1888. She is reported in an August 1893 list of Burin bankers as having obtained one hundred quintals of cod for the summer.

May 1897, the Atlantic Strickland, perhaps being inexperienced in handling the hook and line trawls, was paired with Albert Goddard, a more seasoned dory skipper and the captain's brother. On May 10, *Lily* left Burin, obtained a supply of bait at North Harbour, Placentia Bay and shaped a course for the Misaine. Misaine Bank (or Mizzen as pronounced by many fishermen) was a prolific and much frequented cod fishing ground located off Nova Scotia's east coast. Misaine is about two hundred fifty kilometres from Newfoundland's south coast and the towns of Burgeo and Ramea, both of which played a part in this drama on the high seas.

BURIN BANKERS ARRIVED.

How They Fared With the Fish on the Banks.

SEVERAL of the Burin bankers arrived from the Grand Banks the latter part of last week, and with good fares, too, when it is considered that they, for the greater part, only carry four and five dories. Here are their names and catches :—

The *Ocean Plough*, Vigus, master and owner, 300 quintals.

The *Bloodhound*, Benjamin Hollett, master, Bishop & Co., owners, 240 quintals.

The *Nereid*, Morgan Hollett, master, Robert Inkpen, owner, 190 quintals.

The *Hecla*, Kirby, master, George Inkpen, owner, 150 quintals.

The *Sammy Hick*, John Kirby, master, Bishop & Co., owners, 195 quintals.

The *Jessie*, Weir, master and owner, 160 quintals.

The *Antelope*, Bugden, master and owner, 160 quintals.

Lily, Goddard, master and owner, 100 quintals.

Happy-Go-Lucky, Roberts, master, Keech, owner, 100 quintals.

Artist, Vigus, owner, 150 quintals.

May Belle, Smith, master, Goddard, owner, 120 quintals.

And the *Resium*, William Kirby, master, Bishop & Co., owners, 130 quintals.

List of twelve banking schooners operating out of Burin in August 1893, four years prior to Strickland's ordeal at sea. Most likely *Lily* carried four dories and nine or ten crew. The Goddard business also operated the schooner *May Belle*, Captain Smith. Taken from *Evening Telegram*, August 1893

Lily's crew fished for two days from the nineteenth to twenty-first, but obtained little for their efforts. Captain Goddard ordered the trawls to be taken in and then set in another, perhaps more lucrative, area.

Saturday, May 22, the Dory Strickland and his dory mate, Albert Goddard, rowed out to re-set their lines just before daybreak on a misty morning. Although William Strickland didn't know it at the time, it was the beginning of six days and nights of hardship bordering on horror, coupled with starvation and raging thirst. As he says in his narrative:

In our eagerness to get away we thoughtlessly and foolishly did not see that we had food and water on board our dory. Little did we think we were never to board our schooner again and that there was a fearful fight for life in front of us — the horrors of which have burnt into my brain and being and affected me all my days.

105

Each man thought it would be an hour or two, after trawls were played out, when they rowed back aboard *Lily* for lunch while waiting for fish to get hooked on their gear.

Using the little pocket compass, they rowed toward the mother ship, but it was not in sight — hidden somewhere in the increasing mist. Strickland recalled:

> We rowed all day into a thickening fog and increasing wind. We could see it looked like a night in the dory for us.
>
> When darkness came, the wind was a gale from the southeast and the sea was running high; it required all our skill and strength to keep our boat from filling. At about ten o'clock we heard a steamer's fog hooter but although we pulled frantically in the direction of the repeated sound, which seemed for awhile to be coming nearer to us no lights of a rescuing steamer were seen and the mournful bellowing died away in the dark distance.

This was the first disappointment for the castaways. About midnight they heard another ship's whistle loud and clear, but again their hopes of quick rescue were shattered. This second letdown was, as the already weary Strickland said, "terrible for we were in the darkness and storm with agonizing pangs of hunger and thirst."

Sunday May 23, Dawn on the Atlantic By dawn Sunday, May 23, both men were still battling the raging elements and fighting to keep their frail craft head on into enormous seas. In the small dory they were numbed stiff from cold and suffered severely from cramps. To relieve cramps they had to rub each other's legs and arms to restore circulation.

The second day passed with no letup in the storm howling across the face of the mighty North Atlantic nor any relief from the storms of anxiety raging through their minds. Each man realized the hard facts that with no food and water, rescue would have to come soon or they would never see homes or loved ones again. Their attempts at jokes and positive encouragement seemed pitiful and feeble.

The mother ship is at anchor, the two-man dory filled with fish returns to off load and the weather and seas lie still. When a shroud of fog fell over the banks, only a simple hand-held compass guided the way to safety. In Strickland and Goddard's case, the schooner drifted from its original position or the dory compass was off. Thus began their ordeal at sea.

Strickland, by the end of only the second day adrift, began to notice a change in Goddard and says:

> My companion, as the awful day wore on, was perceptibly weakening. In the late afternoon he lay down in the dory and said he was dying. After awhile I could not even arouse him.

107

William Strickland now had to manage the boat alone. With the bait tub and spare trawl line he rigged up a drag which he hoped would keep the dory into the wind. But it was too short and he had to cut it free, thus he had use his oars all night to keep the boat from swamping. That night only an occasional groan from Goddard indicated he was still alive.

Monday, May 24, The Horizon at Daybreak Overnight the storm abated considerably. Strickland's weary eyes scanned the horizon in anticipation. Although there was no sail in sight, he saw to the westward the purple smudge of high land. With this news he quickly called and aroused Goddard who half rose and nearly regained his senses. Goddard saw the wonderful sight, but neither man recognized what land it was. Gladdened, both men took to the oars, but despite Strickland's entreaties to lie down and rest, the weakened dorymate tried to help the dory along and "it was the last grind at the oars that killed him."

Shocked by death and his own pending end, Strickland said:

> I could neither go any farther nor keep my heavy weary eyes open any longer. I was "all in" for rest and I had to get sleep, but before lying down I remember I somehow fastened a signal to one of the paddles which I raised and secured to the mast pole.
>
> Nature then asserted herself and I slept until sometime in the night during which time the boat must have drifted a long distance.

Night, the Lights of Pass Island When William Strickland awoke and forced himself to stand up, he saw two lights on the land far, far away — on Pass Island, Hermitage Bay, as he found out later.

He checked the body of Albert Goddard, his friend and companion for several days. It was cold and he could feel no heartbeat. Strickland, wanting to get the bearings of the lights, lifted the body enough to get the small compass from Goddard's pocket.

He thought, when laying the body down gently, it gave a long and final sigh indicating the drawing of his friend's last breath. Strickland then looked up into the dark skies and thought of God looking down. "I prayed to Him to have mercy on the soul of Albert Goddard and to spare me to reach land to tell the tale."

Tuesday May 25, A Drink of Blood The morning of the 25th broke dark and dreary — no wind, thick fog and a high sea running. Strickland could not see land now, but rowed from the compass bearings taken the night before. He missed the land although he rowed to exhaustion. In his state of mental anguish he seemed to recall he had heard that a man could quench his thirst with his own blood. He had a knife.

He cut a gash in his arm with his pocket knife and drank the blood. It had the effect desired, for as Strickland remembered, "It really did me good and certainly lessened the agony of my consuming thirst."

During the night a heavy dew fell. William Strickland noticed this the next morning when he glanced at the still body of his friend. "On his oilskins there the dew lay in great drops," and the castaway carefully collected all he could and licked up every drop — remarking that never was water sweeter. It was too little to completely satisfy an all-consuming desire for water, but it helped save his life.

May 26 and 27, South East Rock Uninhabited The day passed slowly. Strickland rowed awhile and rested more until nightfall. He then decided to sleep as much as possible in order to be fresh for the next day — he had a hunch a day or so would bring him to the end of trials and troubles.

All this while he had the body of his companion lying there, but he says, "That did not disturb me. I felt glad his sufferings were over and quite certain that all would end well with me."

The next two days slipped by with the castaway not even cognizant of day or night or how much time had passed. He recalled that he woke early on the morning of May 28th. It

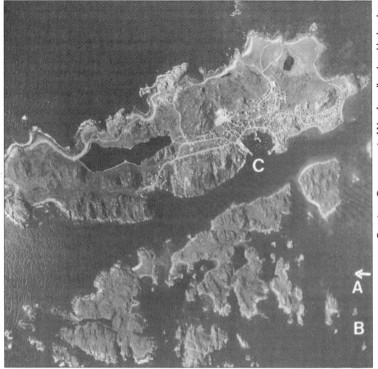

Courtesy Government of Newfoundland and Labrador, Surveys and Mapping Division, 1989

The many islands of Ramea. It was among these islands that William Strickland was finally found, unconscious and near death from exposure. He drifted in a westerly direction from the area of Pass Island (A), over seventy kilometres away, to the South East Rock (B). Strickland was found by William Cutler and taken to Ramea (C).

was a beautiful morning, the sun shining brightly with no fog or wind. To his surprise land was all around and in his delirium he fancied houses on the land. Somehow he found the energy to row steadily to the nearest land. But more disappointments faced him!

> I found this to be a small uninhabited island. (South East Rock off Ramea which is barely above sea level and visited only by hunters for seabirds). Here, however, owing to the heavy sea heaving in, I could not land. It was nowhere possible. I had to put to sea again and in doing so nearly lost heart and hope.
>
> There was the (drinking) water I was dying for — so near

yet out of reach. I think I cried from disappointment and mental pain when I found I could not get ashore.

After William Strickland drifted away from the island, he couldn't row although he was physically able to do so. Now the sun was so hot, it burned his cracked and parched lips and the castaway had to lie face down in the dory for shade. "I do not know how long I lay there in the bottom of the boat," he recalled. "I merely slept until a voice and a shake aroused me."

Mid-Day Friday May 28, Ramea Strickland lived to tell his tale. William Cutler, a fisherman of Ramea, who had sighted what he thought was a drifting empty dory, pulled alongside. To his horror, there was a motionless man on the floorboards, too weak to rise up; and another body.

In as few words as possible — prevented from speaking by exhaustion, a swollen tongue, and cracked lips — Strickland told him who he was and what had happened.

Within a short time he was being well cared for in Ramea and the body of his mate had been reverently coffined. This was shipped to Burin on the coastal mail and passenger boat S.S. *Grand Lake*.

At the turn of the century Ramea, situated on several islands off Newfoundland's south coast, was a long-established town with a population of about two hundred fifty. Constable White, stationed in Ramea in those years, obtained some badly needed clothes at the local merchant's store, John Penny and Sons. Strickland rested for a night in the Cutler home, but found his stay cut short. As he said,

> I was in a terrible plight; my boots had to be cut from my badly swollen feet and I was in such a rack of pain that sleep that night was impossible. It was medical treatment I wanted now and so William Cutler and other friends took me next morning to Burgeo where Dr. Finley McDonald lived.

Twenty-two Days in Burgeo When Strickland landed at Burgeo, he was met by a family friend, Constable Bishop who

111

was stationed in Burgeo at that time. Bishop belonged to Bay Roberts, a town located near Spaniard's Bay where Strickland had lived. The constable took him to the home of Samuel and Ralph Gowers where he rested for twenty-two days.

By this time the news that William Strickland had been lost and was now found reached Spaniard's Bay. Friends and members of the fraternal order to which he belonged, the Loyal Orange Lodge, spared nothing to provide money and means for his journey home.

Before returning to Spaniard's Bay, he first went to Burin to see and to sympathize with the family of Albert Goddard. (The Goddard family name does not exist in Burin today; indeed it is rare throughout Newfoundland).

Strickland remained in Burin for another twenty-two days under the care of Dr. Herbert Smith, who gave him exceptional attention. When the doctor thought his patient was well enough to travel, Strickland continued to Spaniard's Bay.

St. John's, the General Hospital Strickland concluded his epic of heroism and hardship describing the tremendous welcome he received on his arrival home. But his recovery was not complete yet for he said,

> I was far from well though and shortly after my return I was ordered to the General Hospital, St. John's for treatment. The pain in my feet and legs which never slackened to any extent was almost more than I could bear.
>
> For six weeks I was a patient in the hospital where Drs. Shea and Rendell opened veins in my legs and arms in order to bleed chilled blood from them. After this operation I had no more hard pain and rapidly regained my strength so that when I was discharged from the hospital I felt perfectly fit and well.

His Later Years William Thomas Strickland enjoyed excellent health in the years following his ordeal. In 1900, at the urging of friends, he wrote about his experiences and published the above mentioned eighteen-page book entitled *Adrift On the*

Banks in a Dory, subtitled "A True Experience of Adventure and Death in Newfoundland Waters." St. John's businesses placed ads within and a small number were printed; only one copy is known to exist today.

Thankful his life had been spared and that he had not "become a physical wreck or a hopeless imbecile, one or the other, or both," William Strickland turned away from the sea and earned a living as a butcher in a St. John's meat market. He passed away in 1965, age eighty-nine. Fortunately, his daughter, Margaret (Strickland) Grant of Mount Pearl, kept a copy of *Adrift* — in relatively good shape after one hundred years — and shared her father's ordeal with the rest of Newfoundland through this story.

"I really don't know where to look for more details of an old sea story that I've heard bits and pieces of. It's passed on through family traditions. Not much is known." Those words generally come from descendants and relatives of lost mariners who, like myself at times, have reached a wall or standstill in ancestral research. Recently my quest for a missing ship helped me to analyze and to retrace my own process of unravelling a search — a search for names and for answers to a disappearance at sea many years ago.

But where does the first inkling that more information exists come from? Where did that initial contact or source originate? How does one attempt to piece together the circumstances of a relatively unknown disappearance of a ship and its crew? Generally a day, month, or a year provides the greatest clue, but often there are other, more chancy, factors that play a part. I like to think that chance or whim happened to me not long ago and a sea mystery was solved to some degree.

One important aspect of *Raging Winds...Roaring Sea*, and especially chapter eighteen which is a more personal journey, is the inclusion, where possible, of names of seamen, relatives and descendants. To seek out lost ships and crews and to bring both to the light of day is a goal of mine.

18 *A Chance Encounter with the S.S. Sharon*

Port Elizabeth, Fortune, Lapoile

*T*he search for a lost ship, although I didn't know it at the time, began on Davis Island during "Come Home Year" for Port Elizabeth, a resettled community in Placentia Bay. In August 1994 my twelve-year-old son and I decided a trip to the island would become a camping expedition for both of us. We had no direct ties or ancestral connections to the island community, but the outing entailed a short voyage in a passenger boat, tenting overnight in a once-populated and

DEARSON
ARCHIBALD
WHO WAS DROWNED
ON THE
S.S. SHARON
1914
AGED
35 YEARS

SENIOR

This is reproduction of a gravestone from Port Elizabeth, Placentia Bay. Inscriptions indicate a lost sailor and mostly likely a lost ship, but where? under what circumstances?

viable town, an experience in local history and a time for adventure.

On our only full day on the island, August 5, it was foggy; thus our photos of Port Elizabeth and the harbour were not sharp. The closeups, especially of gravestones and the ruins of the church, were fine. I took several photos including one of a large granite marker engraved "Archibald Senior Lost at Sea November 1914 on the S.S. *Sharon*." These were later developed, put away, and would perhaps have been forgotten, but for a phone call six years later.

In June 2000 a phone call gave me a reason to re-examine the gravestone photo. Peter Perham, knowing I researched ships and crews, called from Ontario enquiring if I knew of a vessel called the "Charron", "Sharon", or "Sharron." Since the story had only been passed on verbally through the family, the exact spelling was not clear.

Peter's grandfather, George Nelson Perham, was born in Fortune, but lived in North Sydney. According to family lore, George had worked on a ship that carried iron from Nova Scotia to Wales in 1914. The vessel and crew had never returned and was thought to have been torpedoed by the enemy.

The ship's name rang a bell. I recalled (and later sent to Peter) the photograph of the Port Elizabeth gravestone with "S.S. *Sharon*, 1914" on it. Peter's knowledge of the ship and date agreed with the inscription on the stone. Thus I knew the ship had been lost with least two Newfoundland seamen aboard —Perham and Senior. Now with a ship's name and the date November 1914 firmly fixed, a general search of shipping lists revealed the S.S. *Sharon*, built in Britain and owned by Canada, had left North Sydney November 14, 1914, on her final journey.

Armed with a port of departure and a specific date, I searched — at the Memorial University's newspaper archives — through back issues of relevant weeks in Nova Scotia's *Sydney Daily Post*. On December 16, 1914 the *Daily Post* front page headlines read **Stmr. Sharon Sunk By Mine, Late Theory**. The tragic news said:

The Sydney *Daily Post* of December 16, 1914, theorizes the 3000 ton steamer was sunk by a mine; others speculate an enemy torpedo put her to the bottom.

Town of Port Elizabeth circa 1960s, fifty years after the stone was erected to a lost seaman. Insert shows the United Church, built in 1913. Senior's memorial marker lies behind the church.

The government steamer *Sharon* has been lost somewhere in the Atlantic with all on board and it is believed she struck a mine off the north coast of Ireland...The steamer had a crew of 30, all from the Atlantic provinces. *Sharon*, a new boat costing nearly $150,000, was purchased a year ago from England.

The steamer was commanded by Captain Cochrane. The majority of her crew either belonged to North Sydney or were shipped here, but nearly all of her officers and engine room men were English.

The *Daily Post* gave nineteen names of her roster including George Perham. Family records state that George was one of seven children born in Fortune, Newfoundland, to Martha (Brady) and John Perham. George Nelson Perham married Helen (Green) and had two children: Goldie was born in 1911 and Cecil William Perham, 1912. George was sixty when lost.

Others on *Sharon*'s crew list, subsequently revised to twenty-four men, have surnames common in Newfoundland: Thomas Stacey, leaving a wife and two children;

118

Photo courtesy Maude Senior

Thomas Buffett, three children; George Tobin, a wife and family; Charles Dawe, married and James Spencer, single.

A short while after the information of the loss of *Sharon* and the crew was located, Janet Schlievert of Nova Scotia contacted me to ask if I knew anything about her great uncle Thomas Robert Stacey of Lapoile, Newfoundland. He too lived in North Sydney but was lost on a ship in 1914.

I was able to determine through the *Sharon* list that Thomas Robert Stacey was one of the crew. Family information and birth certificates show that he was born in 1879 at Lapoile on Newfoundland's south coast and married Elizabeth Warr. His two children were Marjorie Adeline, born 1911 and Leonard Roy, 1912.

Several names of the crew — perhaps because they resided in Newfoundland or the maritime provinces — were not listed in the primary source. Omitted was thirty-five year old Archibald Senior, a resident of Port Elizabeth, Placentia Bay. But someday, through a chance finding or by a thorough search, a few more rays of light will be shed on the S.S. *Sharon*'s crew. Names given in *Sydney Daily Post*, December 16, 1914 were Captain Cochrane; chief steward James W. Campbell, born in Scotland, who left a wife and six children; second steward Abraham Jeans, married; fireman William Bonner, wife and seven children; Walter Field, married; Walter P. Walsh, wife and three children; John Bryden, single; Jack McInnis, single; Thomas McLean, single; Henry Caswell, wife and family; William Stirling, wife and four children; Leo Frank, married; Ted Holderness, wireless operator and Perham, Stacey, Buffett, Dawe, Tobin, and Spencer. Field and Walsh were former policemen of North Sydney. Bryden was a well-known hockey player.

This tale of the sea was inspired by Austin Murphy who, in January 1999, sent me his father's story along with four photos of his father, Columba Murphy. Columba had been involved in a poignant epic of the sea aboard the schooner *Nobility*. Through efforts of people like Austin Murphy, who are the storytellers and guardians of family histories, the feats of those who have gone before us will become more widely known.

The story of *Nobility* began for me in 1990 when I first researched and wrote about her sinking. Only two names were available at that time: Captain Amiel Welsh and George Barnes. I decided a short story without the full crew list was better than no story at all; thus a concise version appeared in *Lost at Sea Volume I* (1991). Here in *Raging Winds...Roaring Sea* you get a more fleshed out tale with added detail on who these seamen really were and the hardships they went through. Austin Murphy breathed new life into it when he sent his father's recollections of those stormy months on the broad Atlantic. The *Downhomer* published this story in 1999.

19 Beating the Atlantic

Lawn, Grand Bank

Just a generation or two ago, our forefathers delivered Newfoundland's chief product to the foreign marketplace in Europe, Brazil and the West Indies. The mode of transportation was a wooden schooner, usually powered by sail and human muscle; exporting dry fish was a seasonal operation and that season fell in late fall and winter. It was always a dangerous venture: a small craft, a stormy ocean, a long voyage. Many ships and men disappeared; those ships that returned bore the scars of struggle and the human voices had a story to tell, if they chose to tell it.

The loss of Newfoundland schooner *Nobility* equals many other remarkable tales of the sea, yet it involves local people. There is little information on her long voyage; the

1920 archival newspapers did not carry the story. A few years ago I outlined her loss using details given by one of *Nobility*'s crew: seaman George Barnes of Grand Bank who had recorded a short autobiography of his life. Recently additional information which adds to *Nobility*'s misadventures came from another crewman.

Austin Murphy, a retired marine engineer who lived in Lawn but now resides in Toronto, wrote down a tale of the sea that his father Columba had told him many times. Columba Murphy was shipped on *Nobility* when she left Newfoundland in October 1919 laden with salt cod destined for Spain. By 1919 much fish was shipped overseas in tern schooners which, with three masts and a larger capacity for cargo, were more economical to operate. However, *Nobility* was a ninety-nine ton, two-masted schooner built in 1910. She was owned by merchant Samuel Piercy of Grand Bank. Since most voyages to Europe and back took about four to six weeks, the schooner was outfitted and provisioned with food for such a voyage. Owners rarely provisioned their schooners with extra food and supplies in case their voyage was delayed several weeks by inclement weather.

Six men would take her across the tempestuous North Atlantic. In fact on this final voyage of *Nobility*, the treacherous ocean played havoc on the crew and put the ship on the bottom. Captain Amiel Welsh of Grand Bank, a veteran seaman and navigator, commanded *Nobility* with his mate George Barnes, also from Grand Bank. Barnes had joined the Newfoundland Regiment in 1918, spent sixteen months in Europe and returned from France in July 1919 in time to join *Nobility* on August 4th.

The cook, from Grand Bank or Fortune, was an elderly, crippled man known only by his first name, John. Fritz Keeping, from Fortune and seventeen or eighteen years old, was the youngest sailor aboard. Two crew hailed from Lawn: Columba Murphy and Andrew J. Edwards, both twenty-one.

Nobility's point of departure was New Perlican, Trinity Bay, and in twenty-one days she made the first landfall at Oporto, Portugal. Part of the cargo was discharged and she proceeded to the Mediterranean to land the remainder of the fish at the Spanish ports of Malaga and Barcelona. After leaving the Mediterranean, *Nobility* loaded salt at Cadiz, Spain, to be taken to Piercy's salt storage shed in Grand Bank.

The westward voyage was uneventful until *Nobility* reached a point on St. Pierre Bank, about one hundred eighty miles from Fortune Bay. There they ran into a nor'west gale which tore off the sails and pushed the ship back across the ocean. In the heavy seas *Nobility*'s seams opened and she began to leak. Seawater melted the salt, forcing the men to work the pumps day and night to rid the ship of sea water and brine. The beleaguered schooner was then so light the crew had to put the two anchors and all her chain in the hold for ballast.

Captain Welsh decided to run before the wind for Barbados where the weather was more settled. That run took another eighteen days!

According to Murphy, "We drifted on the Atlantic for eighteen extra days. During that time there was practically no food left on board." Supplies of vital necessities, including tobacco, were low and he recalled that "some of the crew were reduced to smoking tea in their pipes." Mate Barnes said food was so scarce each man was rationed to one slice of bread a day for twelve days. In total the voyage to the Newfoundland coast, back across the ocean, and then to Barbados took seventy-five days.

No doubt drinking water was in short supply as well. Although Murphy and Barnes make no mention of a water shortage, another source, Andrew Horwood's fine and informative book *Newfoundland Ships and Men* (1971) says:

> On *Nobility* their lives were saved by trying to beat the (American) Prohibition Authorities. They loaded salt in Oporto and hid several kegs of wine in the salt. It was seventy-five days after leaving Oporto before they got into Barbados. During the latter part of that voyage they were rationed to all the wine they could drink and still work. (page 123)

Nobility, storm-battered and sinking, soon became a victim of the deep. Columba recalled, "She struck a reef at night off the island of Barbados and became a total loss." The crew abandoned *Nobility* in a lifeboat or dory and viewed the sinking schooner for the last time as they bent their backs at the oars. At nine o'clock the next morning another ship spotted the lifeboat and brought the crew into land.

But their troubles were not over for now they had to find a way to Canada or Newfoundland. They had no money and had saved only the clothes on their backs. Ten days they waited for transportation. In the 1920s a passenger and freight service operated between Halifax and the West Indies, the precursor of the Canadian National Steamship Company, and it was on one of these steamers that the six Newfoundland men, travelling as "Distressed British Seamen," hitched a ride home.

Even on the steamer the shipwrecked seamen had to fight for their rights and for a decent meal. Columba Murphy remembered his partner Andrew Edwards who, although a young man of twenty-one, had served in the Royal Navy during World War One. Edwards lodged a complaint with the ship's Chief Steward. The crew of *Nobility* didn't like some of the food served up, especially sweet potatoes which appeared on their plates instead of regular potatoes.

"That might be good enough for servants or natives of the West Indies," Edwards said, "but we deserve better." The hungry sailors enjoyed the improved fare for the remainder of the voyage.

After a stopover in Nova Scotia, *Nobility*'s crew finally reached their south coast homes — it was the nineteenth of March, 1920. Seven months had elapsed since they left Newfoundland!

Long distance communication in the 1920s was limited, thus it is conceivable relatives on the Burin Peninsula had given up hope for the men believing them lost at sea. But they had survived and lived to laugh about the ordeal. In later years George Barnes, when he sailed into Lawn, visited

Courtesy Austin Murphy

Columba Murphy and his wife standing by the end of his house in Lawn in 1938 about twenty years after his ordeal on *Nobility*. Murphy became the sub-collector of Customs at Lawn

Murphy and Edwards, often reminiscing about the long voyage and hungry days in the winter of 1919-20.

Columba Murphy and his family continued to live in Lawn and he later became the sub-collector of Customs there. In 1954 he moved to Toronto and passed away there in 1968. Andrew Edwards resided in Lawn until his death at age eighty-one. Captain Welsh commanded other vessels until 1935 when he and his crew were lost on *General Gough* en route from Portugal to Newfoundland. Fritz Keeping moved away from Fortune as a young man, but many older people in his home town still remember him. His brother Max, whose name is engraved on the Fortune War Memorial, was killed in World War One.

For George Barnes the ordeal on *Nobility* was not his last encounter with the sea. Seven months later, in October 1920, he was one of the crew of schooner *Nordica* when she was abandoned in the Atlantic. *Nordica* was later salvaged as a derelict, towed into Boston and re-claimed by owners Patten and Forsey of Grand Bank. When the freighter *Administratrix* was cut down off Cape Race in 1948, Barnes and Charlie Fizzard survived. Five of their shipmates were lost.

Thus ends the log of schooner *Nobility* and the arduous voyage of her crew, however it is only with details from men such as Austin and Columba Murphy and George Barnes that such tales of our forefathers are kept alive.

No photo of *Nobility* could be located, but she was schooner similar to *Arcola* (above) shown in 1926 at Shambler's Cove. Those who sailed on *Arcola* in 1926 were Captain Baxter Chaytor (and his son Norman, age seven), Fred Chaytor, Edgar Hoddinott, all of Greenspond; cook Alphonso Hatch of Fortune Bay. *Arcola* was wrecked in 1927 with no loss of life at Partridge Island, near Greenspond.

Crew of *Nobility* (above), c. 1920 Only two are positively identified Columba Murphy, second from left and Andrew Edwards, far right. Note the wheel, left, exposed to the elements and the main boom and gaff.

Around 1959, perhaps spurred by the sinking of dragger *Blue Wave* and her sixteen crew — some of whom were my family friends — I can recall my father, Charles (1898-1979), listing all vessels out of my hometown which were lost with crew. From about 1900 to 1959 he recalled a score of lost ships, their captains and many of the crews' names. Only now do I realize what a resource and fountain of knowledge this man was. No doubt if I had asked him he would have given his own interpretation or theory of the wreck or the disappearance of many Grand Bank schooners.

While he imbued in me a special feeling for my home town, the sea and ships (and eventually an urge to write down as much as possible), I didn't take full advantage of his good memory.

Years later my interest, begun by a fatherly spark, was rekindled and I extended my search for information from Grand Bank to the south coast and eventually to the whole of our seaswept province. So often in my quest I found other people willing to share the stories of their towns, ships and kinfolk. Thus the story is preserved for all. Llewellyn Grimes of Herring Neck sent me the following description of the wreck of the *Jessie*. His grandfather, Elias Grimes, was one of the main characters in this drama of the sea.

20 Down to a Pan of Bread Dust

*J*n February 1903 the coastal mail and passenger steamer S.S. *Glencoe* arrived in St. John's. This in itself was not unusual, but in addition to her regular cargo of goods and manifest of passengers, *Glencoe* also had aboard the crews of two shipwrecked schooners: *Pioneer* and the New World Island schooner *Jessie*. Not much is known of the former, but the crew of the latter, *Jessie*, had been gone for nearly two months and had suffered severe hardships at sea.

Jessie left Gander Bay on Wednesday December 3, 1902,

laden with lumber for St. John's. Her crew belonged to Herring Neck, located at the northeastern extremity of New World Island, Notre Dame Bay: Captain Arthur Holwell, mate George Holwell, Claude Holwell, Elijah Warren, Jeremiah Fudge and Elias Grimes, age twenty-seven. The three Holwells were brothers.

On the day they left the weather quickly deteriorated to high winds and *Jessie* put into Seldom-Come-By, near Fogo, where she stayed two days. The morning of December 5 dawned bright and clear and, in company with three other vessels *Pioneer*, *Nakomis* and *St. Clair*, the schooner sailed again, expecting to be in St. John's within twenty-four hours.

But December weather off Newfoundland's shores is never predictable and by eight P.M. all four ships ploughed through a thick snow storm with winds that increased through the evening to hurricane force. On Saturday December 6 *Jessie* lay to in the storm, but had become separated from the other vessels. About ten P.M. Saturday a tremendous sea swept over the schooner carrying away the bowsprit, jib boom and fore topmast, and breaking off the mainmast about twenty feet up from the deck.

The seas also ripped away every sail and smashed the one boat lashed on the deck. *Jessie* was now helpless in the face of a raging ocean and high winds. About all the crew could do at this stage was to try to steer and to keep the ship's head into the wind. They drifted wherever the winds pushed them.

Captain Arthur Holwell had no idea of his position, for his log had been swept away in the storm and he carried no Atlantic charts nor instruments for mid-ocean navigating. For four days the wind railed and shrieked veering from a southeasterly to a northwesterly wind. Northwest winds increased in velocity and brought with them a thick snow storm.

Jessie iced up. With the added weight of ice and the pounding of heavy seas, seams opened and the schooner began to leak. The six men of Herring Neck manned the pumps, but one pump clogged with sand. When the ship left Gander Bay she carried ten ton in the hold for ballast, but now it washed into the bilges and crept into the pumps.

From Sunday, December 7, the crew realized that food and fresh water were running short. They had left Seldom-Come-By with about forty gallons of water, a bag of hard bread and plenty salt beef, in other words about enough for a two-three day run to St. John's. Now this food was running short and Captain Holwell ordered reduced rations. A day's food consisted of a half pint of water and a piece of hard bread or tack. Furthermore, every twenty-four hours each man gave their half pint to the cook's kettle and hot tea was shared around. The salt beef was useless for they had no water in which to boil it.

This meagre diet lasted for eighteen days, but labour increased. Where they found the energy to work the pump constantly was something that mystified the men. Each said afterwards "We did work hard and never once did we abandon hope."

On the night of Friday, December 12, the lookout sighted a steamer in the distance and the men quickly prepared a flare to attract her attention. But the steamer was too far away and passed over the horizon without noticing the predicament of the floundering schooner.

Dashed hopes! A trial too hard to bear! Such disappointments made work seem twice as difficult and made weary bones seem more tired. Fortunately after this — from December 13 to 19 — the weather subsided to moderate winds and each man caught up on some badly needed sleep.

But this calm preceded another storm. On Friday evening, December 19, a furious gale broke and for the next four days the sufferings of the men on *Jessie* were terrible. They knew their ship was sinking slowly, but such was their hardship they were too tired to work the pumps. Food supplies were so low and scarce that the crew later said, "We were down to a pan of bread dust and about a gallon of water."

One huge sea broke over *Jessie* carrying away the ship's wheel and injuring Captain Holwell's thigh. According to a crewman, by the morning of December 23 he felt that:

The chance of rescue was a hopeless one. [We] worked at the pumps and toiled all that day. In the evening the storm went down, but [we] were in such a state that it made little difference...

That night, however, was the last one aboard *Jessie*. About eleven P.M. they sighted the masthead lights of a steamer. She appeared to be five miles away. Quickly the men mustered around to find a flare. Only a cupful of oil remained in the lantern, but nevertheless the lantern was attached to the broken foremast by a halliard. It was hoisted up and down, up and down in an effort to attract the attention of the passing ship. The steamer seemed to be passing without slowing down, so the men looked around for material for a small signal fire. In the holds were birch or spruce rinds used in the holds to absorb moisture. This kept the fish dry; now it had a dual purpose and helped save the men's lives.

To the unbounded joy of the weary crew, the faint shadow of the ship on the horizon slowly changed course and bore down toward *Jessie*. It proved to be the steamer *Hornby Castle*, bound from Galveston to Antwerp in Belgium. About midnight, chief mate Craven and a select boat crew of *Hornby Castle* drew alongside in a lifeboat.

On board the steamer the Newfoundland sailors were treated with attention and kindness. To their surprise, the captain of the steamer was a Newfoundlander himself — a Captain Jackman. He had left Newfoundland about thirty years before and had settled in the United States. Jackman wished to be remembered to his many friends in St. John's, singling out one in particular, John W. McCoubrey, an old schoolmate now employed in the local printing trade.

On New Year's Day, 1903, *Hornby Castle* reached Antwerp. *Jessie's* crew was sent on to Harwich by the English Consul. Circumstances were not as good in Harwich and the shipwrecked men complained of harsh treatment although they did not say what the conditions were.

Eventually they reached London, England where Captain Joy, Superintendent of the Seamen's Home, cared for them. Joy transferred the seamen to Liverpool where they found a passage to North America via S.S. *Pretorian*, bound to Halifax.

In February, when the coastal steamer *Glencoe* arrived in St. John's from Halifax, the six shipwrecked men had finally and thankfully reached home again. A series of ports — Seldom-Come-By, Antwerp, Harwich, London, Liverpool, Halifax, St. John's — and two months had elapsed since they left Gander Bay in December, 1902.

The crew of the abandoned schooner *Pioneer* also arrived on the S.S. *Glencoe* with the Herring Neck seamen; however the details of her loss have not been recorded. *St. Clair* which left Seldom on December 6 and reached St. John's two weeks later, was driven south by the storm. Elias Grimes gave up working on schooners and found employment as an inshore fisherman out of Herring Neck. He often told others of his harrowing experiences of December 1906. As he said to his grandson Llewellyn, "I didn't think we were going to survive." He passed away in 1957.

There was a short news item on the loss of schooner *Elsie* in the *Evening Telegram*, January 22, 1935, but that brief obituary does not mention the hardships the crew endured. The human element, the personal side of the story came from Joe Osmond of Port aux Basques, now living in Powell River, British Columbia. I am grateful Joe shared specific information of the experiences of his father Cyril who sailed on *Elsie*. Joe had searched the internet for a site on Newfoundland ships, and when our paths crossed there was much sharing of information and anecdotes. He recalled the stories his father often told of the sinking of the schooner, the long cold row to reach land, and the eventual arrival on St. Pierre.

Most of *Elsie*'s crew are gone now, but despite the erosions of time there is no lack of helpful people with fresh information. Joe Osmond is one of those.

21 Ordeal by Frost

Belleoram, Port aux Basques

Elsie, a fast and able American banking schooner, came to an untimely end off Newfoundland. It was a demise that nearly took the lives of seven Newfoundland seamen; such was their hardship and suffering most were unable to work for months after their ordeal.

By 1934 *Elsie* had outlived her usefulness in Gloucester. Times were changing in the United States; new technology and steam trawlers supplanted the wooden vessels and *Elsie* was sold to Captain Levi Kearley of Belleoram. In 1935, commanded by Captain Horatio Kearley, she was engaged in the usual yeoman work: lugging herring, freight, and coal in winter and bank fishing in the summer. *Elsie*, a beautiful ship with sleek lines, had also been a competitive racer in her former life in America, but there was none of that in Newfoundland.

In the 1920s, the awarding of the International Fisher-

Photo courtesy Joe Osmond and Jack Keeping

Elsie in competition prior to her loss in 1935. When this lady of the Atlantic went down, seven Newfoundland seamen fought desperately for their lives.

men's Trophy made headlines in three countries: United States, Canada and Newfoundland.* The trophy was given to the fastest banking schooner in a best of three challenge held off Halifax or Gloucester, Massachusetts. After Gloucester's initial win of the trophy in 1920 (*Esperanto* over *Delawana*) Lunenburg built the *Bluenose*. The Nova Scotian crushed each of the four Gloucester challengers over the next seventeen years — *Elsie* 1921, *Henry Ford* 1922, *Columbia* 1923, *Gertrude L. Thebaud* 1931 and 1938. Only a win of one race in a best of three by *Henry Ford* prevented a total clean sweep. Such was her dominance and glory the *Bluenose* has had her likeness engraved on the Canadian dime for decades.

But this sea misadventure is not about the exploits of *Bluenose*, but of her competitor, the sleek and beautiful *Elsie*. On January 13, 1935, while sailing from Gloucester to Belleoram on Newfoundland's south coast, the old work-horse met the usual spate of winter storms. Five successive days of heavy seas and high winds pounded the schooner

* Although Newfoundland didn't compete, the American entries were often captained by ex-patriot Newfoundlanders.

and on the 18th, she began to leak. Apparently, a plank worked free or as it was termed by Newfoundland seamen, "a plank sprung" — nails worked loose and a gaping hole opened under water.

Horatio and Levi Kearley and five seamen, after pumping for nine hours without a break, abandoned ship at four A.M. in two dories. Four men crowded in one dory while the remaining three were in another. Her crew all came from south coast ports: Capt. Horatio Kearley, Levi Kearley and Jack Poole of Belleoram; Nathan Rose, Burgeo; Cyril Osmond and Harold Sheaves, Port aux Basques and Albert Mills, whose residence is not known.

In temperatures below freezing, and facing a bitter northerly wind which constantly sprayed cold sea water over them, they set out for the nearest land — St. Pierre, forty-eight miles away. During the long pull to land the dory with three aboard was seen to be drifting away; its crew was exhausted and seemingly had given up the fight. This craft was abandoned and all seven crowded into one dory.

By this time, after twenty-four hours of continuous rowing, several men were so cold and drained, they lay down in the bow next to each other for warmth. Those with more strength covered them with whatever was available — mostly oil skins or "foul weather" gear. The ablest managed to get a small pot of fire going in the middle of the boat to keep mitts thawed out, although the fire was too small to fight against heavy frost which now sapped their remaining reserves of energy and will-power.

Several men had given up and were resigned to death, but one or two persevered and kept rowing. Cyril Osmond, age twenty-five, felt stronger than the others and encouraged his shipmates to continue hoping and working.

On the night of January 21, after forty-nine hours of ceaseless rowing and fighting nature's worst elements, they saw a light, but didn't know where they were. It eventually proved to be the French Island of St. Pierre and the light was near a coal pile.

The dory finally reached a beach nearby; Osmond stumbled ashore, close to death through exposure. A watchman or guard from St. Pierre came to greet them armed with a gun. People had been stealing coal from the pile and on the night the *Elsie*'s dory made its landfall, the supply of coal was well-lit and had an armed guard watching over it. The watchman quickly went to find help for the Newfoundland seamen.

The St. Pierrais had to carry the weakened men to hospital; none were able to walk. Those who were released early from the hospital were taken into homes on St. Pierre and given clean clothes, food, and plenty of hot rum to restore life to cold limbs.

According to family tradition, Cyril Osmond and Harold Sheaves were the only two who did not suffer severely frozen hands and feet. In later years when both men got together to talk of their experiences, Sheaves often praised his dorymate for saving his life and probably the lives of all. Osmond was still rowing when the dory reached land. He passed away in 1977 at age sixty-seven.

The captain of *Elsie*, Horatio Kearley, had to remain under medical care for a longer time than the others. His feet were so badly frozen and swollen he was unable to put on shoes until August. He was later lost at sea in 1943 when his schooner *Margaret K. Smith* disappeared while en route from Halifax to Belleoram.

"It's an ill wind that doesn't blow some good," is an old Newfoundland saying and I suppose that's the way it was for me in May of 2000. I was asked to adjudicate a regional Heritage Fair and, although I had several other pressing matters which might have prevented me from doing so, I agreed to help. To my delight I encountered a rare Newfoundland sea story at the fair, told in print by a survivor and ably depicted by Megan Walsh and Byron Holloway, the captain's great-grandson. These students and Boyd Holloway graciously shared the story of shipwreck and survival with me and you.

In a way this chapter, twenty-two, is nostalgic for me for it was one of the last to be written. The stories in this volume were all written separately (as opposed to beginning at page one and writing through to the end) and then fitted into the whole. The selections were either arranged according to the geographic location, story length or variety, thus "Heroism on the Cliff" doesn't appear as the final story in *Raging Winds...Roaring Sea*.

22 Heroism on the Cliff: Bloomfield's Nahada
Bloomfield, Bay de Verde, Spanish Room

It was a final voyage that ended in disaster for the ship and, if not for the determination and stamina of the crew, loss of life would have been the ultimate tally. The vessel was the schooner *Nahada* owned by Benjamin Stead of Musgravetown and crewed mostly by Bloomfield men. Stead used *Nahada* for the coasting trade to carry fish in the fall from Labrador or the French Shore to St. John's. At St. John's she loaded food, dry goods, supplies and general provisions for Bonavista Bay towns. Often she plied the coal route from North Sydney, Nova Scotia to Newfoundland.

Built in 1905 in Smith and Rhuland's yards at Lunenburg, Nova Scotia, *Nahada* netted one hundred five ton and was powered only by sail. As was the local custom for good luck and prosperous voyages, her Nova Scotian builders gave her a name with the letter "a" in it — three a's would bring her more luck. By the 1920s *Nahada*'s registry had passed to Stead, but lady Fortune was not on her side in December 1923.

That fall, crewed by Captain Jesse C. Peddle, cook Edward Penney, seamen Darryl Penney, John Wiseman, all of Bloomfield, Bonavista Bay, Thomas Banfield of Fortune Bay, and Joseph Squires, Broad Cove, Conception Bay, *Nahada* left St. John's with provisions for fishing merchants in White Bay. She unloaded her cargo at Williamsport, Hooping Harbour, Canada Harbour and Englee. In the second week of December, John Reeves Ltd. at Englee loaded about two thousand quintals of salt fish and several casks of cod liver oil aboard *Nahada* destined for St. John's.

Captain Jesse Peddle didn't expect heavy or "dirty" weather; his glass, or barometer, showed no sign of it as he sailed across the entrance to Trinity Bay. But in the evening of December 14 a sudden, intense snow storm materialized seemingly out of nowhere. When the schooner neared Baccalieu Tickle — a body of water which separates the island of Baccalieu from the tip of the Bay de Verde Peninsula — Peddle thought he could reach the shelter of Red Head Cove. Because of low visibility he decided not to attempt to navigate the one and half mile channel or tickle.

Instead he ordered the crew to drop anchor and lower sails outside Red Head Cove. The dangerous area where *Nahada* had anchored had acquired a local name, "The Ship's Graveyard." Although onshore winds lashed the schooner, her anchors held. Seeing the worst danger had passed, Captain Peddle and two crew went below for a much needed sleep; the other three men were put on a four hour watch.

At five A.M. Saturday morning, December 15, as the storm intensified, *Nahada*'s anchor chains broke and the schooner struck the cliffs. She rolled on her side taking water quickly. She was laden with a heavy cargo of salt fish; the seas soon swept over her decks. But the crew had enough time to throw a few personal possessions in the dory and heave the craft over side into the raging sea at the base of the cliff.

Within a moment, the small boat smashed against the

jagged rocks, throwing the men and the few articles of clothes they had saved into the water. Somehow they clung to the slippery rocks and had the presence of mind to carry a length of rope from the dory with them. What faced them now was a sheer wall of rock seemingly hundreds of feet high. There was no choice but attempt to climb it.

Slowly, in the wind and snowstorm, they worked their way up in single file holding and trailing the rope behind for the next man. The first one to the top was told to tie the rope to something firm and pull up the smallest man. Then two men at the top might be able to pull the heavier person. But after scaling twenty-five feet, it was obvious they could go no farther. There were no crevices, hand or foot holds, nor small trees to help them work their way to the top. They had to retreat to the bottom where the sea pounded the narrow ledge they stood on.

There was only one way: sideways and parallel to the base until the cliff showed signs of small ledges or hand holds. Further along, the cliff seemed to be less steep, but the second climb would still be long and dangerous. The six castaways slipped, held on, groped, slipped, but one man, Captain Jesse Peddle, reached the top. Using the rope and bracing himself on the cliff lip, Peddle pulled and each man crawled to safety. Sharp rocks and jagged cliffs cut their oilskins to ribbons.

A new danger faced them. Peering through the swirling snow they could not recognize their surroundings although they knew they were somewhere on the tip of the Bay de Verde Peninsula. Now it was walk until they reached a town, barn or road. After hours ploughing through snow drifts *Nahada*'s crew reached the Bay de Verde railway station. Six hungry, wet, exhausted men with torn clothes frozen onto their bodies stumbled into the station. Normally the office would have been deserted unless a train was coming, but on that day several men from Grate's Cove were there waiting for a branch train.

Soon a warm fire and hot tea revived the spirits of the shipwrecked crew. The station agent contacted Levi Dalton at Bay de Verde to say a ship was ashore, supposedly at Red Head Cove. Dalton asked for volunteers to escort the crew into local homes at Bay de Verde. As the group — ship-wrecked mariners and escorts — trudged through the snow, they were met by men, laden with ropes and reaching poles, headed to the wreck. These men thought some of *Nahada*'s crew were still aboard or clinging to the cliff.

On Saturday night, the Bay de Verde people gave *Nahada*'s crew a "Welcome Party" in celebration of having survived a wreck and reached their town. Sunday morning community volunteers took the crew back to the wreck scene at Red Head Cove. To their surprise there was no wreck at the cove.

"Where did it happen?" they asked. The shipwrecked men could not answer for to them it was only a steep cliff and a small cove. "Could it be Friday Cove?" No, impossible, the men of Bay de Verde thought, for no one could climb those cliffs. But when the group reached Friday Cove, the wrecked *Nahada* lay on the rocks with her canvas strewn around, spars gone and surrounded by her cargo, floating salt codfish. Fortunately owner Stead had fully insured the hull and cargo.

Two of *Nahada*'s crew, John Wiseman and Edward Penney, volunteered to descend the cliff with some Bay de Verde men. Others on the cliff top held the rope. Edward found parts of his gun that he had put in the dory the night before. One part of the gun was jammed in a crevice; another section was further along the rocks. He re-assembled the gun and it stood in the family gun rack for many years.

Little else was salvaged. Their schooner, a home and workplace for many trips, could not be refloated and soon went to pieces at the base of Friday's Cove. Several local men collected a few quintals of fish from the water, but that was all.

On Monday, December 17, *Nahada*'s crew began a series of train-hopping until they reached home three days later: first they boarded the branch train at Bay de Verde for the trip to the Carbonear station. There they spent the night and

Schooner Total Wreck.

RUNS ASHORE NEAR BACALIEU TICKLE.

A message was received from Bay de Verde by Messrs. Bowring Bros. this morning, to the effect that the schooner Nahada went ashore near Bacalieu in the height of the snow storm on Saturday morning and soon

This is how the *Evening Telegram* of December 17, 1923 showed the wreck of *Nahada*.

caught the train to Brigus Junction station. From Brigus, they waited to board the mainline train to Clarenville and continued to Lethbridge, Bonavista Bay. Finally they reached their Bloomfield homes.

Family and friends were overjoyed upon the return of the four Bloomfield men and the other two crewmen. And it was so near Christmas! Festive celebrations began early in Bloomfield that year.

Captain Jesse Peddle, according to the research of his daughter Anna Belle Peddle, next took command of the tern schooner *Earl Grey*. This vessel wrecked on School Room Rock at Seldom-Come-By. Peddle went back to Englee to Reeves' fish premises to help rig the schooner *Nellie Reeves* and to sail her to St. John's with fish. In 1927, four years after his ordeal on *Nahada*, Captain Peddle developed tuberculosis. He retired from the sea and passed away August 20, 1929.

Anna Belle Peddle, with foresight and strong loyalty to her father Captain Jesse Peddle, talked to the last surviving

A model of *Nahada* and the cliffs of Friday Cove. This model showing the wreck of the schooner and the men on the cliffs was Megan Walsh and Byron Holloway's first-place entry in the 2000 Burin Peninsula Heritage Fair. Megan and Byron live in Spanish Room; the latter is a great-grandson of Captain Peddle.

crewman of *Nahada*, Edward Penney. It is through Anna Belle and the late Edward Penney (d. 1986) that we know this story of determination and the physical and mental strength of our seafaring pioneers.

"We Were Doomed to Die." These were words straight from the heart, poignant words describing a shipwreck as told by Fred Parsons of Carbonear. In 1960, in response to a radio program "The Sally West Radio Show" which asked listeners to send in true and curious Newfoundland stories, Parsons submitted his trials on the schooner *Exotic*.

It is not clear if his dramatic tale of shipwreck was ever aired, but the story was preserved and then passed on through the family to son Lew (who was involved in the episode). In turn it went to grandson Scott Parsons, now living in Ottawa. When I told Scott I knew of the vessel *Exotic* since it was owned and had fished out of my hometown around 1900, we both thought of the phrase, "It's a small world, after all."

Scott, knowing that the stories of the strength, determination and resourcefulness of Newfoundland pioneers like Fred Parsons should be perpetuated, gave this story of hardship and courage to me and you. In *Raging Winds...Roaring Sea* and through the voice of Fred Parsons, it is now possible to appreciate the tribulations of those who go down to the sea to work. We might choose to call this tale of endurance simply "The Wreck of the *Exotic*"; perhaps a better title, in keeping with the narrator's struggle to survive, would be "We Were Doomed to Die."

23 "We Were Doomed To Die"

St. Julien's, Shambler's Cove, Greenspond, Freshwater

"I expect, son, it's all over." With these words a father steeled himself as he, his son, and fourteen other people expected to be swept at any second off the deck of the schooner *Exotic*, grounded on an offshore ledge. There was no one on shore to witness the wreck nor to guide the weary people to safety, indeed they could barely make out the high cliffs through the driven snow and mountainous waves breaking over the reef and the schooner.

In the summer of 1933 the Parsons family of Freshwater, represented by three generations — the oldest man Richard Parsons, his son Fred Parsons with his wife, Elizabeth (nee Jones of Upper Island Cove) and two sons, Lew, age two and Sandy, four — fished at White's Arm on the French shore. Following the traditional fishing methods of many Conception Bay fishermen, they were one of several families who left Carbonear or Freshwater on the schooner *Exotic*. As was the usual custom, the "floater" families of Conception Bay fished all summer on the French shore and returned home in the fall. In October when the season ended, Fred's wife and his two small boys went home on the coastal steamer *Prospero*.

In 1960, Fred Parsons wrote down his story of *Exotic*'s last voyage, twenty-seven years after the event. He vividly recalled the voyage, the wreck, and how he nearly lost his life.

Exotic, a schooner of seventy-eight ton, was built in Gloucester in 1888 and eventually sold to Patten and Forsey's business of Grand Bank. About 1925 she was sold to Captain William Kelloway of Perry's Cove, Conception Bay, who used the schooner in the northern fishery. In early November 1933, *Exotic*, with fourteen men and two women aboard, left St. Julien's.

St. Julien's, a spacious sheltered harbour near the tip of the Great Northern Peninsula, was a rendezvous place or departure harbour for most schooners fishing on the French Shore. From St. Julien's fisher families had an hour's steam by motor boat to their "room" or summer residence near White's Arm. These houses and sheds were temporary fishing shacks or cabins. Many fishermen hired a girl to cook for the crew.

That year, 1933, Captain Kelloway was one of the last to leave the French Shore for Conception Bay. Those aboard *Exotic* when she made her final odyssey were the captain and his brother, mate Henry Charles Kelloway; the captain's two sons, Donald and Walter; Henry Charles Kelloway's three sons, Chesley, John and Eugene; the cook Marion Whelan who may have been from Western Bay; Richard Parsons and his son Fred (who wrote down this story of shipwreck); Thomas King, his sons Francis and Fred and daughter Winnie; Gordon Cole of Perry's Cove and Josiah Butt of Freshwater.

On the first leg of the voyage home *Exotic* reached Crouse, four miles below Conche on the eastern side of the Great Northern Peninsula. By this time in November heavy frost and winds were frequent. Crouse harbour froze over and it looked as if *Exotic* might be stuck there for the winter. As Fred Parsons recalled:

> After spending a week there waiting for a fair wind, the wind came up northwest with frost. We noticed we were starting to freeze up with ice all around us and we had to get to work to try get the vessel out of it. After several hours up all night with temperatures near the zero mark we used to lay lines ahead of her and all sails up we finally got her clear of ice in the harbour.

Captain Kelloway could not stay in Crouse and, as winter winds and ice conditions gradually worsened, had to put to sea in a gale of northwest wind. All aboard spent a hard night fighting frost and snow under a single reefed mainsail and jumbo. One man's feet were frost-bitten. When daylight broke *Exotic*'s band of fishermen and crew found themselves off Fogo where the coast was abound with hidden rocks, shoals and breakers. As Parsons wrote, "It was only the guiding hand of Providence," that got them safely through this treacherous area and into Seldom-Come-By, a harbour on the south side of Fogo Island.

> We spent a week in Seldom with gales of southeast winds and snow. I must say here it was always important to make homemade bread enough to last the two weeks journey home. Now after being out for two weeks or more we had all bread gone and had to eat hard bread (tack) with no vegetables.
>
> With the moderation of a northerly gale, we left Seldom on a Sunday after dinner. If we had left four hours before we would have avoided the dreadful time and experiences we went through.

November 26 and the worst winds of winter were about to close in on the band of voyagers, struggling to reach Conception Bay. The schooner reached Cape Freels about midnight, but the wind died out completely. Parsons recalled that it was a calm before the storm, a fatal storm for *Exotic*:

> It wasn't long before the wind came from the southeast and soon there was snow with it. Then it came gale force. Now the skipper's intention was to turn for Shambler's Cove, a harbour not far from Greenspond, Bonavista Bay. First he would make Shoe Cove Point Light and then the harbour.
>
> We finally made the light about four in the morning, but it was too late and before we knew anything there were breakers all around us. There was land ahead and the only thing we could do was to drop anchor. After a little while we discovered we were alongside a breaker or reef.

To hold the schooner from drifting onto the rocks, Captain Kelloway had to let all the anchor chain out, about forty-five fathoms, and this allowed the vessel to drift dangerously close to the inside or lee of the breaker. When the crew sounded water depth, it was very shallow.

Realizing the surly white combers breaking over the shoal would engulf *Exotic* at anytime, Kelloway ordered the crew to hoist out a small boat. All climbed aboard at great risk to their lives. Knowing an attempt to row away in the mad seas would upset the boat, they tied it to the schooner, allowing the boat to drift astern. In this position, tossed by heavy seas and with their vision almost totally obscured by a raging blizzard, they waited for daylight.

The decision to get off the schooner was a wise one, for as Parsons said:

> ...By this time the decks of *Exotic* were awash with waves sweeping over her for we were anchored on a lee shore. After waiting awhile daylight came. To our dismay we couldn't see any place to save our lives. All we could see were mountainous cliffs with seas breaking about 50 feet up in cliffs.
>
> We all thought we were doomed to die. I remember now my father was standing beside me on the deck and the

words he used were 'I expect it is all over.' I thought of
home, my wife and my two little sons I wouldn't see any
more. But suddenly there was a little clearing in the snow
and we could see a little cove where we thought there was
a possibility of saving our lives.

Captain Kelloway noticed the vessel began to drag her
anchor and it was clear that within minutes she would drift
on the rocks. Thus he decided to get the people back aboard,
slip out *Exotic*'s chain, and run for shore. In his recollections
Parsons wrote that he could hardly describe the situation
with the seas breaking right across this little cove. Yet it didn't
seem as bad in the middle where they shaped the short and
final course for the beleaguered schooner.

It must be remembered too that many of the sixteen
people about to abandon *Exotic* and to run a gauntlet for their
lives were not seamen, but fishermen. And for the two girls,
this was a new and terrifying experience.

> When we let her go and *Exotic* got to this bar, she ran
> aground. First we thought she would stay there but not for
> long. Before we knew anything a big sea struck her right in
> the stern and drove us in over the reef. She went in a little
> gulch. We started to try to get ashore.
> It was now snowing. You couldn't see a hand before you
> and it wasn't long before we were all ashore with only a few
> personal belongings saved. But before we left her we cut
> her foresail away to make some sort of a shelter.

Bringing the sail with them was a piece of foresight that
saved their lives. As Fred Parsons, the writer of this remarkable tale of hardship, recalled, the canvas sail became a tent, a
rough and crude shelter that kept the heavy frost and snow
from the survivors. Without it, some would have perished
during that long cold night. They had no food, except a loaf
of bread soaked by sea water, and only brook water to drink
although the night was too cold to make much use of ice
water.

When the wreck finally ground to a halt on the rocks,
Kelloway dropped the port anchor and made two lines fast to
the shore. The two girls, as it was related afterward, were "of

true British stock and took their orders bravely and obeyed promptly."

Kelloway and his band of wet and cold survivors discussed their location, believing they were not far from the town of Shambler's Cove, about six miles overland. But they were in no condition to reach the people living there, for as Parsons recollected:

> We weren't ashore very long before the vessel broke up and we made a fire at the mouth of our camp with wreckage according as it came ashore from the wreck. This was in the morning before daylight and we walked so far away in hopes of finding someone, but the storm was so bad we would have to turn back for the camp.
>
> We had very little to eat and oh what a night we spent! Sometime that night the wind changed to the northwest and froze by all creation.

Finally, after a long cold night, daylight broke. It had stopped snowing and visibility improved. Parsons, Captain William Kelloway and two others set out overland for Shambler's Cove. There was no path and the group had to slog through deep snow over bogs and hills, through woods and across brooks. When they reached a pond, walking over the ice was a little easier.

The first signs of civilization were telegraph poles which they followed, and this led to a road. Eventually they saw the first house of Shambler's Cove — which co-incidentally was the home of Captain Daniel Bragg, an old friend of some of *Exotic*'s band. Shambler's Cove, now an abandoned community, then had a population of sixty. Captain Bragg, who was well-to-do, had a large, grand house. Parsons recalled:

> In no time his good woman had a good feed before us which was greatly appreciated. (In later years he always remembered the kindness shown by the Braggs and said that the meal and cup of tea was the best he had ever tasted.)
>
> After we told the story, Captain Bragg had the news spread around Shambler's Cove that *Exotic* was lost at Fox Harbour Cove.

Bragg had a large motor boat which he soon had ready to go get the remaining part of our crew and to gather up what few belongings we had salvaged. With ourselves and two or three men from Shambler's Cove we went by boat to the place where our vessel was wrecked. The people from Greenspond and Newport heard of the wreck and were already on the scene. It wasn't long before they had holes cut in the side of *Exotic* trying to get fish that was aboard.

Richard and Fred Parsons soon gathered their families' few belongings from the schooner and left the scene saying,

Courtesy Government of Newfoundland and Labrador, Surveys and Mapping Division

Shambler's Cove (B) where *Exotic's* crew and passengers walked to safety. Rescuers came to their aid from (Loo Cove) Port Nelson (A) and Greenspond (C). The schooner was wrecked at Fox Harbour Cove (D). The causeway to Greenspond Island was built in 1983.

Photo courtesy Gordon Sparkes.

Home photo courtesy MUN Archives

The Newfoundland coastal steamer *Home* aground (later refloated) in 1926 at Fogo. Captain Thomas "Tommy" Hounsell (insert) of the S.S. *Home*, brought the shipwrecked passengers and crew to Conception Bay.

"We bid adieu to the old, old *Exotic* and that experience never to be forgotten." He finished his amazing tale of survival by thanking God for safe deliverance and for his return to his family again.

Those men of Shambler's Cove and area who went to rescue the remaining castaways waiting in a crude tent at Fox Harbour Cove were: Daniel and Eldon Bragg, Peter Ford, Tom Carter, Moses Maidment, Silas White, Edward King and Baxter White (originally of Port Nelson, but living in Shambler's Cove) with his motor boat and crew. Magistrate and wreck commissioner J.B. (Job Brenton) Wornell and Constable Richards of Greenspond arranged to have the shipwrecked people put up in local homes — the families of Walter Carter and Jesse Bourne. Seven days after the wreck the coastal steamer S.S. *Home*, Captain Tom Hounsell, brought them to Conception Bay.

Fred Parsons passed away in 1970, ten years after recording his story on paper and thirty-seven years after the event. His son, Lew, who fished on the Labrador and sailed on *Exotic* on her last voyage from Conception Bay to St. Julien's, lives in Portugal Cove. Captain Kelloway's version of the wreck was published in the *Evening Telegram* on December 8, 1933.

Not often does a researcher and writer of sea stories find reliable and clear documentation describing the last moments of a wreck. Usually details come from detached and brief newspaper clippings. If the date, place and description from newspapers can be augmented with anecdotal and personal experiences, the writer is fortunate indeed.

A special tale of the sea was shared with me in January 2000 when a friend, Lance Blackmore, originally from Port Union, allowed me access to a 1948 typewritten account of the loss of sealer *J.H. Blackmore*. The two-page single-spaced description had no title except the heading "The story of the accident..."

I was equally grateful to obtain sharp photos of Captain Johnny Blackmore's vessels which he had built and sailed over the years. As well, I located a lengthy article in the March 12, 1948, edition of the newspaper *Fisherman's Advocate* which verified many details in the personal report.

After I learned of the many facets of Captain Johnny's exploits at sea, I knew the ship story and the brief biography of his life was one to be written and shared.

24 The End of the J.H. Blackmore
Port Union, Spillars Cove, Elliston

About thirty seconds after Fred Blackmore left her, the vessel was in the cliff and that cliff was over 100 feet high, straight rock about two miles from land, Spillars Point, near Cape Bonavista. The sea would take the boat and beat her against the rocks and she would come back unhurt, but one wave took her and put her so far in the cliff that she hooked. When the water ran out she came down with a terrific bang. There was a crash like thunder. Some of the crew heard it half a mile away and knew it was the end. (Excerpt of 1948 report entitled "The Story of the Accident")

*J*errifying in its might and majesty, the sea, on the night of Tuesday March 9, 1948, claimed for its own the well-known sealer *J.H. Blackmore*. Captain John Blackmore of Port Union not only owned and skippered the vessel, but also designed and built it. Motor vessel *J.H. Blackmore* (or just "Blackmore" as she was commonly called) had been steaming for one night when crushing ice fields trapped her off Cape Bonavista. The crew escaped by a miracle and walked over the ice floes to the town of Elliston, on the eastern tip of the Bonavista Peninsula.

Captain "Johnny" John Hann Blackmore, who had forty-six men including his son Fred with him, left Port Union in *J.H. Blackmore* on Monday morning intending to pick the remaining crew at Pound Cove, Bonavista Bay. Captain Blackmore steamed out to view ice conditions off Cape Bonavista, intending to skirt the field.

However, the whims and winds of nature wheeling the ice in and out trapped *Blackmore* off Spillars Cove, a little southeast of Cape Bonavista. Growling and grinding, the rafted ice, estimated by Captain John to be three fathoms thick, pushed the two hundred twenty-five ton sealer slowly to her death.

Built in Johnny Black's (or Blackmore's) Cove, Port Union, in 1943 by Captain John Blackmore, his two sons George and Fred and eight other men, *J.H. Blackmore* was 138 feet long and had a 240 hp Fairbanks-Morris engine. In her first summer of work (and in the summer of 1944 and 1945) she was chartered by the U.S. Army for service in Greenland. It is a point of interest that in 1944 in Greenland waters she had reached a location fifty miles farther north than any of explorer Peary's ships had reached during the famous Arctic expedition when Peary discovered the North Pole. In the winter of those years *Blackmore* resumed the seal hunt for the Blackmore business of Port Union.

Now, caught in the spring ice of 1948, she was doomed. *J.H. Blackmore*'s end came when the propeller caught in the ice and this stopped the engines. Twenty-two hours later the ice had pushed *Blackmore* within fifteen feet of a point of rock projecting from the ice like spires of a church. Each spire had an abyss with great ice rafts running out between them.

In the water free of ice around the spires, it became possible to get the engines going again, but heavy seas at the base of the cliff drove *J.H. Blackmore* on the jagged rocks.

Moments before, the crew hastily threw a few belongings into four dories and launched the boats on the seaward side of the vessel. The last man to leave jumped into slob ice as the seas flung the doomed *Blackmore* against the unforgiving rock. The demise of the sealer is described in the 1948 report:

> Fred (John Blackmore's son) was the last person to leave. His father cried out to him to come on, so Fred turned off both engines. He wanted the *Blackmore* to die in peace and quiet. He turned off the lights and ran up the ladder. Passing his own room, he grabbed a bag, left the light on, closed the door and ran on deck.
>
> He heard his father say, "Come on Fred, that's all you can do." So he jumped over the side down on the ice where his father and three other men were waiting in a dory. Then seconds later, her head was in the rocks and the force of the seas and ice was too great.
>
> Fred Blackmore said, as he watched her go down, that the light in his room was the last to go out. He got all the men together and tied four dories in a line with so many men to a dory. He gave one man a pocket compass, showed him a course to go by and sent him ahead.

Danger on the Ice Meanwhile the crew with the four dories fought nature's elements to stay alive. The weight of the dories was about all they could pull over the uneven piled-up ice. It was ten P.M. when they left *Blackmore* and twenty minutes to one Wednesday morning when they reached a cove called Square Gulch south of Cape L'Argent, one and a half miles from the scene of the wreck.

Once in the cove, the men were stuck. They couldn't retreat by boat and they faced high rugged cliffs. Despite the

Ice dwarfs *J.H. Blackmore* shown above with bridge master Billy Rideout standing on the wheelhouse. This is the type of rough ice faced by forty-six men when she was lost on the Spillars rocks off Spillars Cove, near Bonavista, on March 9, 1948. Some of the other sealers on *J.H. Blackmore* at this time were Charles Rose, Roland Dyke, Frank Harnum, Ken Samson of Port Union; Daniel Piercey, Caleb Edgecombe, Forward Janes, Little Catalina; Des Peters, Melrose.

shelter of the cove, the swell heaving in made their position dangerous. Above them were steep cliffs around 180 feet high and covered with ice. This, according to "The Story of the Accident" is how they conquered the ice and cliffs:

It was dark and stormy with thick snow falling and drifting. Captain John Blackmore wanted to walk, but because of his age and the trauma of seeing his vessel dashed to pieces, his son would not let him. He put John in a dory and made him stay there until they reached land. Sometimes the crew would walk and then sink in the slob forcing them to lie across the ice to pull themselves out.

They nearly lost one man. He got jammed and the dory slipped away from him. He went down to his armpits in heavy slob. Fred and two or three other men went to their waists in the attempt to get him free. After nearly three hours they reached Square Gulch and a ledge of ice just large enough for the men to stand on. After they were there a few moments, three big waves came in and cleaned the cove of the slob ice they had just left. Had they been on the sea ice at the time, it would have been the end of all.

Now they had to face an icy cliff about 180 feet straight up. One of the crew had thrown a new coil of light strong rope in one of the dories — this helped save their lives. Another man who was used to climbing had stabbers (ice picks) on his boots. He scaled the cliff. Two other men went behind him preparing a route with knives and gaffs and the three brought the rope to the top.

At the top of the precipice lay a large rock; they tied the rope securely around it and one by one, each man below scaled the cliff. Fred Blackmore was the last up sending his father up with two more men — one ahead to help pull him and one behind to push. Before Fred left the bottom, he tied four dory paddles together and sent them to the top. These would serve as a stretcher for his father if needed. Finally all clothes bags and a few other items saved from the *J. H. Blackmore* were sent up.

At the top of the cliff they rested awhile. Someone had a cake in their clothes bag; another had a bottle of rum. So they all had some and then started to walk to Elliston, the nearest town. Fred carried the makeshift stretcher with him right to the door of the first house. Thank God they all escaped, but it was miracle.

It was Alfred Johnson of Little Catalina who volunteered to scale the cliff and another man followed behind him. According to a story in the newspaper Clarenville *Packet* November 1, 1999, written by Anne Barker, Alfred Johnson recalled:

The hardest thing about getting up was the ice, which was all over the rocks, but I zigzagged back and forth to get the best way up. I had a gaff and that helped me.

Once I got to the top, I looked for a place to tie the rope. At first I could see nothing there...but this rock as big as a table. I went around and around it with the rope and I tucked some blackberry trees in so the rope wouldn't cut. When this was done, I told them they could come up and

Photo courtesy Lance Blackmore, Grand Bank/Port Union

In 1940 Captain John Blackmore built the one hundred eighty ton *Nanuktut* (above) which he sold the following year to a North Sydney firm. In 1943, he helped finish the *J.H. Blackmore*.

they all came one after another. Then we hauled up all the clothes bags.

Within ten or fifteen minutes after the last man was off the narrow shingle beach at the bottom of the cliff, a large sea swept the cove and smashed the dories to pieces. Captain Johnny Blackmore always claimed if it had not been for Alfred Johnson, who found a way to climb the cliff, the entire crew would probably have been killed or drowned.

J.H. Blackmore's men reached Elliston at four A.M. Wednesday morning. By noon they returned to Port Union by truck. At the time of his death-defying ordeal, Captain John Blackmore, born in Newtown, Bonavista Bay, was sixty-six and had already earned a reputation as a man who helped build Newfoundland's maritime tradition.

The story of his first command at age twenty-six illustrates his courage and character. He was looking for a schooner to use in the Labrador fishery. The only thing available was an old damaged vessel, his father's fifty-one ton *Ethel Blanche* lying a derelict on the beach. He took that, repaired her and sailed for the Labrador coast.

Not finding any fish on the usual grounds, he kept going north until he reached Eclipse Island and Cape Childey where neither he nor his crew had ever been before. But he found the cod, filled his vessel and returned safely, the only ship to get a load. From that point his success at fishing, sealing and shipbuilding gradually improved. He lost but one schooner, the *Corsair*, which broke her chains in a 1939 storm and went ashore in Twillingate. After the loss of *J.H. Blackmore* Captain John obtained another vessel the following year. This was Clarenville-built *Newfoundlander* and it too went to the bottom at the ice fields about five years later. In 1948 he was bestowed with an OBE — member of the Order of the British Empire; he passed away in 1970.

In the summer of 2000 I became aware of a terrible Newfoundland gale when I read Eric Larsen's book on hurricane damage in Galveston in September 1900. I realized September 2000 was the anniversary of the same storm which ravaged parts of Newfoundland and that prompted me to research and to write.

A section of this account contains the crew lists of wrecked vessels. Initially I was reluctant to present this long list, but quickly realized the names would not only add authenticity, but would be a boon to family historians and genealogists. When the story was published in the *Evening Telegram*, it did not have my suggested title (The Deadly Face of Nature) but carried the more misleading "Isaac's Storm." It was Isaac Cline's storm in the southern United States, but in Newfoundland the September gale had no name.

25 *The Deadly Face of Nature*

Northern Peninsula, Carmanville, Straight Shore

Back then it was a face with no name. Time was when the disastrous hurricanes originating in mid-Atlantic and howling through the United States were not called Hurricane Andrew, Dianne, Nancy or any other first name. That trend appeared in the 1950s.

But the hurricane of September 1900 caused so much damage and hardship that it was later labelled "Isaac's Storm" after the meteorologist Isaac Cline who erroneously predicted it was of no consequence. When the 135 mph winds hit Galveston Island, Texas (where Cline lived) on September 8 the storm surge and waves destroyed half — roughly 3,600 — of the homes and buildings in Galveston and killed over 8000 people. (After the flattened Galveston was re-built, a sixteen kilometre seawall was constructed to protect the low-lying city from storm surges.)

Before the death-dealing calamity hit Newfoundland, it brought hurricane force winds to Chicago and Buffalo, killing

Map of the track of "Isaac's Storm" of August 29 to September 13, 1900.

several loggers and riverboat men in the area. Winds downed so many telegraph lines that communication throughout America's Midwest came to a standstill.

On September 12, 1900, the storm took several lives as it crossed Prince Edward Island, then moved stealthily with killer intent over Newfoundland. It first ravaged St. Pierre-Miquleon, the French islands near Newfoundland. According to J.P. Andreiux's book *Shipwreck at St. Pierre*:

Today with modern navigation and weather reporting, there is time for warning of these fierce storms, but at the turn of the century no such warnings were given. On September 13, 1900, such a tornado struck St. Pierre.

On the ships sunk in St. Pierre harbour no lives were lost,

but nine fishing schooners at the offshore banks had nowhere to seek shelter. They failed to return to port and 120 French fishermen drowned.

The death toll of Newfoundland vessels and lives was high. Two factors accounted for this: no one knew the hurricane was coming, and a great number of schooners were gathered in one area of Newfoundland. Scores of fishing ships concentrated near the tip of the Great Northern Peninsula, as it was fall, and they were finishing up their voyages or travelling east to home ports.

On the evening of Thursday, September 13, the winds — now reduced to an intense and localized gale — lashed Newfoundland's coast, particularly the east side of the Great Northern Peninsula. Between Belle Isle and Englee forty-two fishing ships were driven on the rocks; about half were never refloated or repaired.

Initial reports from William Cunningham, the Justice of Peace at Tilt Cove, indicated no loss of life. But by September 20, this changed when he received news that five men were lost at Pacquet, a fishing harbour located on the north shore of the Baie Verte Peninsula.

That vessel — carrying eighty quintals of salt cod — had anchored near Pacquet. People on shore saw the drama unfold, but were in no position to render assistance. The crew, probably thinking the ship could not withstand the force of wind and waves, attempted to reach land in a small punt. It upset, drowning all five.

The schooner rode out the gale and was later brought into Pacquet harbour safe and sound. The only identification found aboard was a powder horn inscribed, "William Over, Bonavista."

Cunningham's report listed several wrecked schooners and their masters: *Northover*, Captain Nelson, Old Perlican; *Fairyland*, Captain Samuel Wiseman, Bonavista and Henry Clapper's boat of Little Bay Islands. Coombes' vessel of Round Harbour, near Twillingate, first reported missing, was safe.

Reports of other ships lost came from Musgrave Harbour.

In a letter to the *Evening Telegram* dated October 18, 1900, Reverend W.A. Palmer — writing from Musgrave Harbour — observed that "the fishery was worse than it has been for years," and that the recent storm of September 13 was terrific and would not soon be forgotten by people on the Straight Shore.

One vessel from Hant's Harbour grounded at Cat Harbour (Lumsden) to total loss. The men saved their clothing, but the wreck was sold at public auction. The dismasted and broken hull of the small schooner *Maggie* was located and towed to Doting Cove where it was beached.

Most distressing was the loss of the schooner *Goodwill*, Captain John Carnell of Carmanville. Owner George Carnell's two sons sailed on *Goodwill*, both married with one child each. Three other seamen, one married with three children, were also lost on *Goodwill*. Relatives and friends waited for its arrival from Labrador, but there were no sightings of the overdue vessel.

A few days after the day of the great storm, a mainmast, rigging and sail were picked up at the Wadham Islands. George Carnell knew the debris was from *Goodwill*. Then, part of the companionway housing with a knife attached to it drifted in. The knife had the words 'John Carnell' cut into it.

With this evidence the last ray of hope vanished. It was believed *Goodwill* struck Duck Island and all five crew perished there. Rev. Palmer's appeal to the local paper asked for donations of money, food, or clothing to help the widows and orphans. Only one body was ever recovered.

At Twillingate, the thirty-five ton schooner *Combat*, owned by E. Small of Moreton's Harbour, had just returned from the Labrador. She moored at Pathend and had part of her cargo discharged when the storm came on. *Combat*'s anchor chains parted and she drifted in at Shoal Tickle on the southside of Twillingate harbour. Her rudder was carried away and her keel strained.

At three P.M., September 13, the vessel *Six Brothers*, owned by Simeon Young of Twillingate, broke her anchor chains and struck the rocks at Phillip's Landwash on Twillingate's southside. The keel and hull were extensively damaged. Job Brothers of St. John's learned that their schooner *Emerald*, carrying three hundred quintals of fish, was totally destroyed at Quirpon, a town on the extreme northeastern tip of the Great Northern Peninsula.

Tugela, built in 1900 by Josiah Manuel of Exploits Island, was lost somewhere between the Great Northern Peninsula and Exploits Island with two crew aboard — George Foote and Chelsey Manuel, who was the youngest son of owner Josiah Manuel.

In his report of September 19 to Thomas J. Murphy, the Acting Minister of Marine and Fisheries, Cunningham listed many of the ships' crews landed at Tilt Cove by Captain Cross of the tug *D.P. Ingraham*. Cross confirmed forty-two vessels wrecked along the coast and *D.P. Ingraham* picked up several shipwrecked crews. Among them were the following:

Pandora, Bonavista — Captain George Harris, William Little, Lewis Harris, Joseph Saint, Eli Paul, Fred Harris, Adam Harris and Dorcas Fifield;

E.S. Mackey, St. Brendan's — Captain James Mackey, Patrick Mackey, Peter Mackey, Frank Mackey, John Hogan, James Batterdon, Joseph White and Mary E. Hogan;

Sea Slipper, Happy Adventure — Captain John Moss, Fred Moss, Hettie Moss, Allen Moss, Alfred Elliott and William Watkins;

May Flower, Little Bay Islands — Captain Henry Chapter, Joseph Goudy, Charles Morey and Philip Morey;

Kate, Bonavista — Captain William Sutton, Joseph Cuff, William Dominey, John Hill, Gideon Cuff and George Bishop;

Silver Spray, Happy Adventure — Captain Robert Powell, James Powell (Jr.), James Powell (Sr.), Alfred Powell, Edley Powell and Francis Powell;

Ocean Traveller, Fortune Harbour — Captain John Quirk, Dennis Dunn, Joseph Cooke, Thomas Croke, Patrick Croke, Morris Quirk, William Quirk, Michael Burn, William Burn and Ellen Dunn.

Four crews, who did not have the money or resources to pay for their trip to Tilt Cove, also came by *D.P. Ingraham* under order of the Poor Commissioner. Relieving Officer John Moore undersigned or authorized payment for their voyage:

Eseleus, Change Islands — Captain John Parsons, Ted Parsons, Allan Oft, Albert King, Silas Drew, and Andrew Boreme;

NonPareil, Change Islands — Captain Thomas Day, John Folkes, Nathaniel Crane, John Crane, Elias Day, Samuel Oke, and Edward Coleman;

Mary Ann, Fair Island, Bonavista Bay — Captain Samuel Wiseman, Robert Wiseman, George Wiseman, John Wiseman, Samuel Wiseman;

First Trial, Botwood — Captain James Antle, William Antle, Thomas Jacobs and John Peterson. Mary Fitzgerald of Coachman's Cove, who was a lady cook on the Labrador fishery, also arrived on the *D.P. Ingraham*.

Two other Newfoundland ships disappeared around this time; of course the exact day of their loss is not known. According to the Edgecombe family of Catalina, the schooner *Lillydale* of Catalina discharged her fish at St. John's on August 23, 1900 and had returned to the banking grounds off the Avalon Peninsula. On September 13 other vessels saw her lights early in the evening as the windstorm intensified, but *Lillydale* disappeared before daylight. Two of her crew were Captain William Edgecombe and Simon Russell Edgecombe of Port Union.

P.K. Jacobs, a thirty ton schooner owned in St. Lawrence by Robert Reeves, sailed blindly into the storm. She had been to St. Pierre to load bait and left September 12, 1900, for the banks. From that point on the fifty-eight foot schooner disappeared. Her crew, all of St. Lawrence, was lost: Captain Joseph Jacobs, James Reeves, George Poole, William Turpin, Paddy Murphy and Pikes — Louis, Archibald, Samuel and Robert. Two were sons of Albert Pike; another, the son of Manuel Pike.

One hundred years ago, a terrifying face of nature slipped away from our island and headed north, arcing across the seas off Greenland and finally disappearing from human knowledge. The effects of the storm that nearly annihilated Galveston is now the subject of Erik Larsen's book

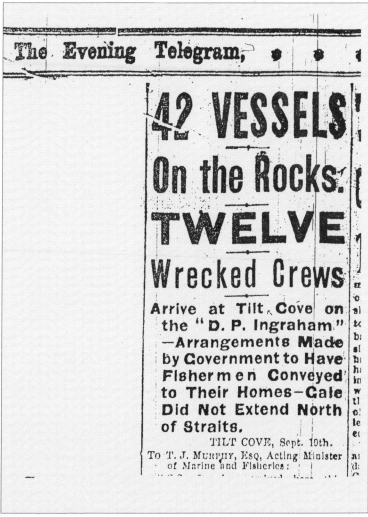

This *Evening Telegram* headline indicates the tremendous loss of ships and cargoes in the September Gale of 1900.

165

Isaac's Storm, published in 1999. In Newfoundland that storm, which also destroyed ships and took lives, had no name.

In 1963 at age eighteen, I attended Teacher's Preparatory Summer School in St. John's. In August I was assigned a position at Philip's Head, Notre Dame Bay. Philip's Head had a two-room school and I enjoyed my tenure there immensely. The following year I was assigned to teach at Botwood near Philip's Head.

Philip's Head had an unusual attraction — the remains of World War Two military bunkers. Of course in 1963 I didn't know I would eventually write about the purpose for those bunkers. It was not until the summer of 2000, nearly forty years later, that I researched the ships that the guns protected. One ship was the S.S. *Geraldine Mary* which must have steamed past Philip's Head headed to Botwood, twenty-five years previous to my stay there. Ironic too, is the fact that when *Geraldine Mary* sank in 1940 the only passenger killed was a man who had a great vision and plan for Newfoundland.

26 Victim of War

Botwood, Philip's Head, Grand Falls

The paper carrier S.S. *Geraldine Mary* was a familiar sight in Botwood harbour for ten years. Several times a year she plied her way up along the northeast coast, into Notre Dame Bay and the narrow arm of Bay of Exploits and then the friendly confines of Botwood. Her role as a transatlantic supply ship taking paper produced in the Grand Falls mill began in Botwood in 1930. With the outbreak of World War Two her work put her in jeopardy. *Geraldine Mary*'s foreign port was across the Atlantic, but hostile German submarines lay in wait for European bound convoys and preyed on Allied shipping.

Owned by Anglo-American Development Company (A.N.D.), *Geraldine Mary* was used to transport Newfoundland newsprint to Europe. Built in 1924, she was fitted with specially-designed bows for ice-breaking. In addition to modern quarters for officers and crew, the vessel had six staterooms that could accommodate twelve passengers. The ship, with its fifty-five thousand ton capacity, had been employed in Newfoundland from 1930 to 1940 and operated out of Botwood in summer, Heart's Content or St. John's in winter depending on ice conditions.

With Captain Syme in command, the steamer, loaded with newsprint, left Botwood on July 19, 1940 to join a convoy out of Halifax on its way to England. The convoy, code-named HX60, unwittingly sailed straight into the jaws of three German U-boats under orders to attack North American ships. Sub 52, commanded by Otto Salman and lying in wait about three hundred miles off the Irish coast, upped periscope on August 4 and saw the unarmed *Geraldine Mary*.

A few Newfoundlanders travelled on *Geraldine Mary*: passengers Guy Harvey, Grand Falls, and two women of St. John's: Mrs. Gordon Warren and Miss Gordon Baird. Gordon Baird, the daughter of the late David Monroe and Emma Baird, was on her way to England to marry Derrick Bowring of the Newfoundland Royal Artillery. She had an unusual first name of Gordon (also a family surname) and was, at first, assigned a room on the port side of *Geraldine Mary* usually reserved for men. Then the ship's purser realized Miss Baird was a woman and gave her a room on the starboard side.

Mrs. Warren travelled to England to join her husband, also in the Royal Artillery. Dorothy St. John, who had been a governess or nanny in the home of Gerald S. Doyle (of the renowned Gerald S. Doyle Radio Bulletin), was returning to England. Businessman H.C. Thomson travelled on *Geraldine Mary*. He was born in England, but lived in and visited Newfoundland often. Crewman Alex Crawford, the son of Mr. and Mrs. H. Crawford of Long Pond Road, St. John's, had been on the ship for two years and had a brother Harry in the Royal Air Force.

One passenger on *Geraldine Mary* briefly described the attack:

At three A.M. on August 4 we received warning of subma-

Errata

In reformatting some pages in *Raging Winds ... Roaring Sea*, text from pages 169 and 170 was accidently eliminated. We have prepared this errata sheet so you may have the entire text, as the author originally submitted it.

rines and got up and dressed. After about two hours it was thought that danger had passed and all retired again.

We were asleep when the attack came. Passenger H.C. Thomson was on the side of the ship where the torpedo struck and was fatally injured. There was a rough sea at the time of the explosion and we (the passengers and crew) were five hours in the lifeboats before we were picked up by a friendly warship (*Sandwith*).

Geraldine Mary, filled with paper which absorbed water, sank very slowly, giving the crew considerable time to launch the lifeboats. Unfortunately and ironically only one passenger slept on the port side (Miss Gordon Baird had been given a room on the starboard side) where the torpedoes slammed into that side of the ship — eighty-four year old H.C. Thomson. He was an industrialist and active proponent of the establishment of a Newfoundland free port, a zone within a port where import-export regulations and restrictions are lifted in order to encourage international trade. Thomson had business connections with the A.N.D. Company and campaigned vigorously for a free port and a trans-shipment base to be situated in Mortier Bay on the Burin Peninsula. Because Thomson advocated so strongly for Mortier Bay, which had little fog and a deep spacious harbour, he was known as "Fog Free Zone" Thomson.

During the early part of World War Two the threat of German subs was very real around the coasts of Newfoundland, as evidenced in Bell Island Tickle where the enemy sank

rooms that could accommodate twelve passengers. The ship, with its fifty-five thousand ton capacity, had been employed in Newfoundland from 1930 to 1940 and operated out of Botwood in summer, Heart's Content or St. John's in winter depending on ice conditions.

With Captain Syme in command, the steamer, loaded with newsprint, left Botwood on July 19, 1940 to join a convoy out of Halifax on its way to England. The convoy, code-named HX60, unwittingly sailed straight into the jaws of three German U-boats under orders to attack North American ships. Sub 52, commanded by Otto Salman and lying in wait about three hundred miles off the Irish coast, upped periscope on August 4 and saw the unarmed *Geraldine Mary*.

A few Newfoundlanders travelled on *Geraldine Mary*: passengers Guy Harvey, Grand Falls, and two women of St. John's: Mrs. Gordon Warren and Miss Gordon Baird. Gordon Baird, the daughter of the late David Monroe and Emma

Courtesy Maritime History Archives

Botwood paper carrier *Geraldine Mary* sunk by enemy action off the coast of Ireland. Two other ships with Newfoundland connections were sent to the bottom around the same time: one was *Humber Arm*, no casualties among her crew. Three crew hailed from Port aux Basques (one of whom is known at this time — John Gillam Spencer) and seventeen from Bay of Islands. S.S. *Davidson* was also torpedoed on July 10, 1940 and all crew, including Ray Stoodley of Grand Bank and William Pickford, survived.

Photo Robert Parsons

At the outbreak of WWII Canadian soldiers constructed elaborate heavy artillery stations, bunkers, concrete tunnels and living accommodations (similar to those at Cape Spear, near St. John's) at Philip's Head in the Bay of Exploits. They were built to protect ships entering and leaving Botwood. The tunnels and gun turrets are accessible to the public today.

Baird, was on her way to England to marry Derrick Bowring of the Newfoundland Royal Artillery. She had an unusual first name of Gordon (also a family surname) and was, at first, assigned a room on the port side of *Geraldine Mary* usually reserved for men. Then the ship's purser realized Miss Baird was a woman and gave her a room on the starboard side.

Mrs. Warren travelled to England to join her husband, also in the Royal Artillery. Dorothy St. John, who had been a governess or nanny in the home of Gerald S. Doyle (of the renowned Gerald S. Doyle Radio Bulletin), was returning to England. Businessman H.C. Thomson travelled on *Geraldine* four ships. To protect paper carriers like *Geraldine Mary* as they steamed up the Bay of Exploits to Botwood to load, the Canadian government built a strategic artillery station at Philip's Head, located about four kilometres from Botwood.

Construction took place from 1939 to 1943. The complex eventually included a 700-foot underground passageway, complete with booby traps, eleven rooms, a three-storey observation tower, and gun pads for two 4.7 inch guns. These guns, with muzzles about ten feet long and shells weighing 149 pounds, were fired at subs several times in the early 1940s, but by 1943 were seldom used. The station, equipped with three large searchlights, was situated about ninety feet above the water on the high point of land, or the head, within the town.

Throughout its active occupancy, up to 570 Canadian commandos or soldiers were stationed and trained at Philip's Head. In the Atlantic, Nazi submarines sank several paper-carrying ships: *Geraldine Mary, Esmond, Imogene, Humber Arm,* and *Ungava*.

In 1975 through the initiatives of Johnny Stride (who was labour foreman during its construction and in whose home I boarded in my own tenure at Philip's Head in 1963-64) of Philip's Head, the gun station was restored and today is a community park and a tourist attraction.

This, the final chapter in *Raging Winds...Roaring Sea*, really began in August of 1999, when Edith Burrage of New Perlican sent me a version of this story. The basic details of the loss of the *Flash* have been written and published in several other places. What I have added is the human element, that of women, children and relatives who waited at home and worried while their seamen fought the raging Atlantic.

Slowly, these stories of our past, our people, and the events which shaped our rock-girt island are slipping away. Time, failing memory and the inevitability of death are thinning the ranks of island storytellers. This tale "In God's Own Time" helps sustain the memory of our pioneers and one particular facet of their lives — the sea. The trail of memories (as noted above) began when Burrage recorded what she knew of a sea epic that had been passed down through family and kin.

Tantalizing bits, these retellings are — often just enough to whet the appetite for more. In obscure shipping lists one can often read various snippets of marine misadventures and of lives lost at sea, but the summaries are bare and lack the personal, anecdotal information that brings a story to life. These vessel obituaries where they bid a brief farewell, merely make those interested in sea stories long for the more fleshed-out tale. Such a tale is that of the people of New Perlican who waited and despaired.

I entered "In God's Own Time" in the 2000 provincial Arts and Letters contest, the non-fiction prose category, and it received Honourable Mention. Unlike the other stories in *Raging Winds...Roaring Sea* this one is endnoted as submitted for the competition. I feel the documentation has value even for the casual reader; hopefully it will show where the sources from which the facts (as I perceived them) are derived.

27 In God's Own Time

*J*ust a generation or two ago, our forefathers delivered Newfoundland's vital supplies of food, dry goods, tools and materials around our island coast. The mode of transportation was a wooden schooner, usually powered by sail and human muscle; the coasting trade was a seasonal operation and that season fell in late fall and winter when the fishing season was over.

Coasting, as it came to be called, was always a dangerous venture: a small craft, a stormy ocean, a long voyage from St. John's or other large ports to the more isolated bays and towns. Many ships and men disappeared; those ships that returned bore the scars of struggle and the human voices had a story to tell, if they chose to tell it.

December twenty-third, the day before Christmas Eve and traditionally called "Tibb's Eve" in many parts of Newfoundland, was generally a time for families to celebrate and to prepare for the upcoming festive season.[1] But work on small coasting vessels goes on — they load or discharge supplies, pull out of port and slog the ocean in their attempt to bring winter supplies to waiting families. There is no time to celebrate.

So it was for a Trinity Bay schooner, the fifty ton *Flash* out of New Perlican, Trinity Bay.[2] She left Harbour Grace with a load of general cargo in late December 1876; local stories claim she was due in New Perlican on December 23.

Flash carried five crew — Captain Charlie Matthews, Richard Callahan, Levi Smith, John Howell and Richard Seward — all of New Perlican. Their loved ones and relatives, seeing the fine weather and knowing the schooner to be seaworthy and well-founded, waited patiently in New Perlican believing *Flash* would be in port by December 23.[3] It was not a lengthy journey: north in Conception Bay to Baccalieu Tickle, around the tip of the cape past Grate's Cove and down Trinity Bay to finish the voyage — about one hundred miles by sea.[4]

It became a long wait for those in New Perlican; days stretched into weeks. The adage, "While there is no hope from the grave, there is hope from the sea," would be sorely tried in the anxious days ahead. In January a report in the newspaper *Harbour Grace Standard* gave a glimmer of hope that nothing disastrous had happened to the schooner:

> - *No confirmation of the report of the loss of the "Flash" at Baccalieu, as announced in a late number of the* Advocate, *has been received here...*[5]

Meanwhile on that December day in 1876, the *Flash* was laden with cargo and slipped her lines heading for New Perlican. As Captain Matthews sailed out of Harbour Grace, he surveyed the weather — no wind to speak of, clear skies — and shaped his course for home. Within four hours they were abeam of Baccalieu Island, off the southeast tip of Bay de Verde Peninsula and somewhat between Conception Bay and Trinity Bay.

"Excellent progress," said the skipper. "We'll be home for Tibb's Eve. I allow before dark today we'll be tied on to Bemister's Wharf."

"The wind is picking up, Skipper!"

"Swinging around northeast. Don't look too good now, boys."

Within an hour or two, a vicious winter northeasterly, snow and low temperatures pounded the crew and ship with ever-increasing intensity.[6]

In New Perlican too, on that night of December 23-24, the storm struck with a destructive strength and folks knew their schooner was out in the weather, trying to reach home.[7] Situated on the south side of Trinity Bay and north of Heart's Content, New Perlican was first settled by families involved in logging, shipbuilding and the 'laying up' or caring for

Photo courtesy Government of Newfoundland and Labrador, Surveys and Mapping Division

Overhead view of New Perlican (1995): a Church of England clergyman visiting in 1764 noted eight families at New Perlican of which half were English, half Irish. Other early family names include Burrage, Callahan, Cotter, Fisher, Grant, Hobbs, Matthews, Peddle, Penney, Piercey, Seward, Smith, Warren and White. The first Newfoundland Census of 1836 lists a thriving community of more than 200 people.

vessels in the winter. The harbour provides a well-sheltered anchorage. Tradition has it that two unrelated families of Heffords were among the earliest year-round settlers.

New Perlican was well-known for its fine shipbuilders: William Pittman, working with the Lester-Garland business of Trinity, began a shipyard in New Perlican and he or his descendants managed it until the 1920s. When Garlands sold out, John Bemister and later Reuben Bemister, managed the shipyard and shipping business. Today, with decreasing population brought about by a decline in shipbuilding and little fishing, the town has about 250 people.[8]

Flash, built by the Pittmans in New Perlican in an area known as Pittman's Dock, was owned by Reuben Bemister.[9] When talk surfaced around kitchen tables in New Perlican, many voiced the opinion that *Flash* was most likely overwhelmed by the December gale while rounding Baccalieu. The snow that covered the windows and land and the wind that rattled the homes, most likely had battered and subdued the small schooner.

Wives and families were heartsick. Christmas celebrations ceased; family and friends spoke in hushed voices. Small children sensed a subdued atmosphere. Older, veteran seamen shook their heads, daring not utter aloud their thoughts of five men lost at sea.

Rather than give up hope, they said, "Sure, perhaps she drifted off. Wait a few more days. There's hope from the sea."

As the weeks passed into January and lean and hungry February roared in, bereaved families of the five crewmen had to resort to charity to survive. Extended family and townspeople provided food, clothing and fuel. Charitable drives began in several towns nearby. But most people had given up the thought of ever seeing the men again, all except John Howell's wife, Christina.

"Somehow, somewhere," she told all, "the *Flash* is afloat. John and the rest of the crew have ridden out that awful December storm."

Aunt Chrissie, as she was affectionately known in New Perlican, firmly believed that her husband, through the mercy of the Divine, would be reunited with her again. "In God's own time, in time, someday. In God's time," she confirmed her faith.[10]

Then on February 24, two months after *Flash* set sail, an extraordinary event happened. The doorman in a Harbour Grace town hall where a fund raising concert was being held for the stricken families of the lost ship shouted, "Stop! Stop! Oh God be praised! The crew of the *Flash* are in town and all alive and well!" To appreciate this dramatic change in circumstance, it is necessary to backtrack for a moment.[11]

In January 1877 *Arctic*, one of John Munn and Company's fleet of foreign-going vessels, left Harbour Grace for Barbados. Under the command of Captain Alex Parsons, *Arctic* carried salt fish to Antigua. The story of how *Arctic* found Captain Matthews and rest of *Flash*'s crew and brought them home is best related by *Flash*'s captain as he told it in the February 24, 1877 edition of *Harbour Grace Standard*.[12]

Captain Matthews' Ordeal On the December day *Flash* left Harbour Grace, Matthews reached Baccalieu Tickle, but when the storm came on suddenly, he gave the narrow and dangerous passage a wide berth and was pushed across to the north side of Trinity Bay. *Flash* fell to the leeward seven miles from Catalina. When the wind increased, the vessel lost its mainsail and the furious gale ripped up the rest of the canvas.

On the next day, with winds veering south, Matthews tried again to reach Baccalieu, but came within eight miles of land. Winds veered, carried away the remaining sail, and again subjected *Flash* to the mercy of the whitecapped ocean. Sea constantly broke over the vessel and she was a complete wreck: the deck parted aft and opened from the side about three inches. As they drifted farther and farther into the open ocean, the crew tried in vain to patch the gaping seams with blankets. Pumps were useless and soon gave out.

Water had to be bailed by hand from the cabin. After four days of sleepless nights and ceaseless labour *Flash*'s crew saw they could not keep the vessel free of water. They resigned themselves to death by drowning. Then in the distance and to the leeward they spotted another ship: the *Iris* (as it was eventually learned) bound to St. John's from PEI with produce. *Iris* too had been driven off course by the same gale that accosted *Flash*.

Matthews immediately and as best he could, kept *Flash* in line with this ship. When it came close enough, he made a signal of distress. *Iris'* captain replied that he would take them aboard if they could rescue themselves. As the captain explained later, *Iris'* lifeboat was too heavy to get over the rail and into the sea.

What was to be done? Matthews had a small boat on deck which they had scuttled in order to prevent it from being washed away; that is, the boat was lying under water while secured to the deck or over the side. This alone gives some indication of the state of the wallowing *Flash*. Somehow Matthews and his crew plugged the holes, bailed the water out and got in.

The captain of *Iris* placed his vessel in position to act as shelter to the leeward as *Iris'* crew stood on deck with heaving lines. When the small boat came near enough for the lifelines to reach, it was pulled to the side of the rescue ship and *Flash's* men clambered aboard.

By then *Flash* already had three feet of water in the holds and sank soon after; the crew was frostbitten and feeble, but slowly recovered. *Iris* was not able to sail to Newfoundland and drifted south until it reached Barbados. There the shipwrecked crew was cared for by an agent of John Munn and Company; then sent to Antigua to join Munn's vessel *Arctic*, bound for Newfoundland.[13]

Communication in those days was limited; relatives in New Perlican knew nothing of the rescue of *Flash's* crew, their transfer to *Arctic* and the unanticipated voyage to the West Indies. When *Arctic* arrived in Harbour Grace, the first order of business for the survivors was a walk to the telegraph office. Henry Shortis, the Morse operator, contacted the cable station at Heart's Content and sent this telegram of happy news to New Perlican:

"Crew of *Flash* alive and well at Harbour Grace!"[14]

It is a matter of coincidence that on the day and hour *Arctic* arrived in her home port a benefit concert was about to begin in Harbour Grace in the Total Abstinence Hall, once one of the town's largest facilities.[15] The "Mohawk Minstrels", a group of employees of the Anglo-American Company cable station operators in Heart's Content who performed light opera and musicals, scheduled a musical play in aid of distressed families in New Perlican. Some years later, Newfoundland balladeer Johnny Burke was a member of the Mohawk Minstrels. Two of his songs, "Clara Nolan's Ball" and "The Kelligrew's Soiree", were performed in 1889 by the Minstrels.[16]

On that February day in 1877, the Total Abstinence Hall was filled to capacity and £ 31 had been collected. Suddenly the doorman announced the news that *Flash*'s crew, once given up for lost, had arrived in town and was about to enter the hall. Needless to say the audience went wild and jumped up in their seats to see the men who now appeared as if raised from the dead.

It was a miracle unfolding before their eyes. Pianist Isaac Angel struck up the music to "Praise God from Whom all Blessings Flow" while the crowd sang, shouted and cheered. Many stood on chairs just to get a glimpse of the men.

The next day *Flash*'s crew set out for New Perlican accompanied, according to some sources, by the Mohawk Minstrels and a brass band led by Paddy Cramm. When they arrived, one can only imagine the joy and excitement in New Perlican.

No one was happier than Aunt Chrissie Howell who had never given up hope that her husband would come home from the sea. She knew that glad day would come in "God's Own Time."[17]

Sources: In most Newfoundland folk tales, especially those which have an amazing or strange turn of events, there is usually a kernel of truth. Thus, in an effort to cross reference or verify a family story surrounding the miraculous appearance of the crew of *Flash* — a tale which had been passed down through several generations — I went to archival papers for January-February 1877. In the Newfoundland Reference Room, A.C. Hunter Library, I located Captain Matthews' story from the *Harbour Grace Standard*. A brief announcement from the January paper revealed that no one was really sure if *Flash* had been wrecked near Baccalieu.

That the light opera musical group "Mohawk Minstrels" of Heart's Content performed a benefit concert for the lost crew is substantiated by Burrage's story, the newspapers of the day, and through Newfoundland reference material.

References:
1. *Dictionary of Newfoundland English* Story, G.; Kerwin, W.; et al, editors. St. John's, 1982
2. Information taken from the Newfoundland Registry of Shipping, Marine Archives, Elizabeth Avenue, St. John's
3. Written correspondence from Edith Burrage, New Perlican in August 1999
4. Chart and map consulted in Map Room, QEII Library, Memorial University
5. *Harbour Grace Standard* mid-January issue, 1877
6. Captain Charlie Matthews' story as told in *Conception Bay Advertiser* February 24, 1877 and retold in *Harbour Grace Standard* February 24, 1877
7. Burrage, August 1999
8. *Encyclopedia of Newfoundland and Labrador* "New Perlican" Harry Cuff Publications, St. John's
9. Newfoundland Registry of Shipping, Marine Archives, Elizabeth Avenue, St. John's
10. Burrage, August 1999
11. *Family Fireside* newspaper, December issue 1940
12. *Harbour Grace Standard* February 24, 1877
13. Captain Charlie Matthews' story as told in *Conception Bay*

Advertiser February 24, 1877 and retold in *Harbour Grace Standard* February 24, 1877

14. Burrage, August 1999
15. *Encyclopedia of Newfoundland and Labrador* "Harbour Grace" Harry Cuff Publications, St. John's
16. Details of the musical group "Mohawk Minstrels" came from several sources: chiefly *Encyclopedia of Newfoundland and Labrador* "Music", and written correspondence from Edith Burrage, New Perlican
17. Burrage, August 1999

Individuals and Businesses

Keans, Capt. Edward, 92
Kearley, Capt. Horatio, 133
Kearley, Capt. Levi, 133
Keeping, Capt. ?, 73
Keeping, Fritz, 122
Keeping, Max, 125
Kelloway, Chesley, 144
Kelloway, Donald, 144
Kelloway, Eugene, 144
Kelloway, Henry Charles, 144
Kelloway, John, 144
Kelloway, Walter, 144
Kelloway, Capt. William, 144
Kenny, William, 85
Kerton, ? (wireless operator), 6
King, Albert, 164
King, Edward, 150
King, Francis, 144
King, Fred, 144
King, Thomas, 144
King, Winnie, 144

Lady of Dorcas Society, 39
Langdown, Arthur, 1
Langdown, Priscilla, 2
Ledingham, John, 66
Lilly, Inspector ?, 23
Little, William, 163
Long, Capt. Leonard, 92
Lundrigan, Thomas, 14
Lewis, Capt. ?, 7

MacDonald, Dr. Allan, 80
Mackey, Frank, 163
Mackey, Capt. James, 163
Mackey, Patrick, 163
Mackey, Peter, 163
Maidment, Moses, 150
Manuel, Chesley, 163
Manuel, Josish, 163
Marsh, Francis, 2
Marsh, Joseph, 1

Matthews, Capt. Charlie, 174
McCarthy, James, 53
McCoubrey, John W., 130
McCue, Philip, 63
McCurdy, Capt. ?, 34
McDonald, Dr. ?, 111
McElroy, Mrs. Thomas, 8
McInnis, Jack, 120
McKenzie, Simon, 15
McLean, Thomas, 120
Mercer, Elijah, 16
Mercer, Josiah, 16
Mercer, William, 16
Merrigan, Ted, 85
Mills, Albert, 135
Mokeler, Richard, 46
Moore, John, 164
Moore, Thomas, 53
Morey, Charles, 163
Morey, Philip, 163
Morris, Capt. Francis, 99
Moss, Allen, 163
Moss, Fred, 163
Moss, Hettie, 163
Moss, Captain John, 163
Moulton, J.T. (business), 84
Mudge, S., 40
Murphy, Columba, 121
Murphy, Paddy, 164
Murphy, Thomas J., 163

Nelson, Capt. ?, 161
Newell, Samuel, 85
Nichol, Sergeant, 24
Nickerson, Capt. William L., 63
Noel, Nat, 48

O'Brien, Brien, 46
Oft, Allan, 164
Oke, Samuel, 164
Osmond, Cyril, 133
Osmond, Joseph William, 51
Otterson, Peter, 85

Over, William, 161

Palmer, Rev. W.A., 162
Parsons, Capt. Alex, 178
Parsons, Fred, 143
Parsons, James, 90
Parsons, Capt. John, 164
Parsons, Lew, 143
Parsons, Richard, 144
Parsons, Sandy, 144
Parsons, Selby, 80
Parsons, Ted, 164
Patey, Elihu, 100
Patten and Forsey (business), 125,144
Patten, J.B. (business), 78
Paul, Eli, 163
Peddle, Capt. Jesse C., 138
Penney, Darryl, 138
Penney, Edward, 138
Percy, Robert, 50
Perham, George Nelson, 116
Peters, Des, 154
Peterson, John, 164
Pickett, Gilbert, 32
Pickford, William, 169
Piercey, Daniel, 154
Piercy, Samuel (business), 78,122
Pike, Archibald, 164
Pike, Louis, 164
Pike, Capt. Reuben, 53
Pike, Robert, 164
Pike, Samuel, 164
Pine, Capt. Ben, 59
Pine, Capt. Frank, 60
Pittman, William, 176
Poole, George, 164
Poole, Jack, 135
Powell, Alfred, 163
Powell, Edley, 163
Powell, Francis, 163
Powell, James, Jr., 163
Powell, James, Sr., 163
Powell, Capt. Robert, 163
Prim, Capt. Joseph, 65

Index of Towns and Ships